¡ÁNDALE, PRIETA!

A LOVE LETTER TO MY FAMILY

YASMÍN RAMÍREZ

Cinco Puntos Press
an imprint of LEE & LOW BOOKS Inc.
95 Madison Avenue, New York, NY 10016
leeandlow.com

Edited by Lee Byrd
Book production by The Kids at Our House
The text is set in Crimson Text
Manufactured in the United States of America by Lake Book

First Edition
10 9 8 7 6 5 4 3 2 1

Library of Congress Cataloging-in-Publication Data

Names: Ramirez, Yasmin, 1981- author.
Title: ¡Ándale, Prieta! / by Yasmín Ramírez.
Description: First edition. | New York, NY : Cinco Puntos Press, an imprint of Lee & Low Books Inc., [2022] | Summary: "A memoir by a Mexican American woman that doubles as a love letter to the tough grandmother who raised her"-- Amazon.com.
Identifiers: LCCN 2020035628 | ISBN 9781947627550 (paperback) | ISBN 9781947627567 (eBook)
Subjects: LCSH: Ramirez, Yasmin, 1981- | Mexican American women authors--21st century--Biography. | Authors, American--21st century--Biography. | Grandmothers. | New York (NY.)--Biography.
Classification: LCC PS3618.A465 Z46 2022 | DDC 818/.603--dc23
LC record available at https://lccn.loc.gov/2020035628

Mira, Ita, lo hicimos.

PART ONE

FINDING ITA

ONE

I SPENT FIVE years selling lingerie at Nordstrom in the elite Highland Park neighborhood of Dallas. Though that season of my life is peppered with countless memories, I don't really remember the very first time I helped a woman find the correct size prosthesis for her bra. But I've never forgotten the conversations I had with these women before we began each fitting—almost always the same.

Every time I stepped into the black-and-white paisley-printed fitting room to help them, they'd ask right away, "Can't your manager help me?"

"I am the manager," I'd reply.

Pinched eyebrows, pursed lips.

I was in my mid-twenties, a baby in the eyes of most fifty-year-old women. What did I know about the scars that marked their bodies?

They hesitated to take their blouses off.

"Please sit down," I would invite them. "My grandmother had breast cancer," I would begin. "I grew up watching her adjust her prosthesis in mastectomy bras. I know what the scars look like. It won't shock me. I just want to make sure you're comfortable. If at any point you're not I can step out. Or we can stop."

They'd relax. And when they took off their blouses and allowed me to see the pink scars on their chests, I didn't blink. We talked about Ita as I measured across and around their naked torsos.

"How old was she when she got cancer?"

"Forty. I wasn't born yet, but my mom told me about it—how she changed after."

"Was it bilateral or unilateral?"

I'd slip a robe around them so they wouldn't have to sit in the fitting room facing the mirror naked from the waist up when I stepped out to get the flesh-colored prosthesis and mastectomy bras.

They made me think of war veterans. *Where did you serve? What unit?* But instead, *Was it one breast or two?*

"Uni."

Ita had a jagged scar because it had happened long ago when surgeries weren't so sophisticated. I told them about the special bra shop, Margie's, in downtown El Paso where I watched a woman fit Ita while I sat on the fitting room floor holding her purse. She always complained about the ugliness of the bras. They nodded, understanding, as I lined the fitting room with various nude bras they would never find at Victoria's Secret.

"You don't have t-shirt bras?"

The smooth molded cups would do nothing for them. "No. The seams in each of the bras give shape to both your real breast and the prosthesis. The seams even things out, and they'll only show a little bit under snug t-shirts."

Oh.

"There should be prettier lingerie for breast cancer survivors," I'd say.

"Your grandma must be glad she has you to fit her."

The women would leave with a bag full of silicone or gel prostheses and nude bras with pockets to hold their new breasts in place. They would thank me. Some of them even hugged me.

I didn't tell them I never got a chance to fit Ita.

TWO

AT THE TIME it seemed normal. Later I learned that most grandmas don't teach their granddaughters to fight, especially when their granddaughters are only in first grade.

But there she was, holding her clenched fists in a fighter's stance in front of me. "Si alguien te pega ¿qué vas a hacer?"

So—what *would* I do if someone punched me? "Punch them back?"

"No empieces nada, pero no te dejes, ¿eh?"

"Okay, Ita. I won't start anything, but I won't let myself get pushed around either."

"Y más vale que ganes, ¿eh? Porque si no, cuando llegues a la casa te voy a poner otra chinga."

I stared at Ita, letting her words sink in. I really don't think she would have given me a chinga if I lost a fight, but just in case, I was definitely not going to lose.

Earlier that day at Lamar Elementary, Eric had pulled my braid. He'd pulled so hard, the red plastic bolita at the crown of my head snapped. *Pop!* Mrs. John, my teacher, asked me what had happened when I came in from recess, my hair all over. I told her my bolita had broken. I stared up into her crinkled blue eyes when she asked me again, but I told her the same thing, and this time I looked down.

Every morning, music from a Juárez radio station crackled through the house. Ita hummed along to the boleros, ballads, and other stuff they played while she brushed and braided my hair. My hair was long, way past my waist, thick black waves of wires pointing in every direction. She brushed it with a metal bristle brush, tiny steel soldiers standing at attention, ready for battle. I'd heard people tell her that I had *cabello de india,* but I didn't understand what about my hair made it Indian? It didn't look like the hair on the pretty ladies in the cowboy movies we watched.

She brushed and brushed until every tangle was out, pulled my heavy hair into a tight ponytail, smooth and perfect at the crown of my head, then braided it into a thick three-strand rope. Sometimes my eyes watered from my hair being pulled so tight. My eyelids pulled at an angle from my temples. I held my head high and braced against the pulls, my neck stiff to make the process easier.

But today after recess, I'd kept my face down, staring at the brown wooden desktop, my loose braid pulled to the right side of my face so I wouldn't have to see Eric, wouldn't have to see anyone. *I hated Eric.* I knew Ita wouldn't be happy when I got home, my hair loose and disheveled.

But now, there I was, braid repaired, standing in front of Ita, my eyes wide, while Estela Casas on the 6 o'clock Channel 7 News reported loudly in the background. Ita sat on the edge of the worn brown paisley couch, so I was her height. We'd moved the green marble Formica coffee table out of the way for more room. The gold cross she always wore lay shiny on her chest. It rose and fell with her breath. She wasn't saying anything. I stared at her face, waiting. She stared back, sin sonrisa, her arched brows squished to the center. I squished my eyebrows and lips to match hers.

She took up a boxer's stance again, but this time she opened her palms toward me. I stood ready, left foot in front, right foot back like she'd told me . . .

"No. Mira, Prieta."

I glanced at my feet and then back at Ita as she stood up. She placed her feet the same as mine but bent her knees a little. "Porque así—" Mine were locked. She reached over and shoved me. I lost my balance. "Tienes que plantarte bien para que no te tumben."

I put my feet back where they'd been, this time with my knees bent like hers.

She shoved me again. I stayed put.

"¡Eso!" She smiled and sat back down on the couch.

"A ver, las manos como le enseñé."

She held up her hands and made two fists, her fingers curled into her palm, her thumb wrapped around her bent fingers. The green center vein on her right hand bubbled when she clenched her fist into a tight knot. A nurse had popped her vein trying to put an IV in. It had been that way ever since.

"Amacice bien el puño para que no se quiebre la mano." She showed me her tightly clenched hand. "Mire."

I made my hands into fists too.

Ita's face was soft. She seemed young, not like the other

grandmas at school who looked like raisins. She held her clenched fist out for me to see. She didn't have any make-up on—we were staying home—it was a school night. The skin on her face glistened from her face cream. I smelled its mixed floral scent. She looked at my hands and nodded. I wondered if, when I hit someone, my nails would hurt my palm. I wanted to ask her but didn't. She held both hands face out on either side of her chin.

"Óra sí, pégale."

I stayed still, my fists clenched to either side of my chin the way she showed me. I didn't want to hit her.

"¡Pégale! ¡Pégale!" She waited some more, nodding her head, her eyebrows raised. "*¡Ándale, Prieta!*"

I was frozen in a fighter stance.

"Mira, Prieta, así."

She reached out and opened my damp clenched hands and put them to either side of my face, and she punched, tapping at each hand. I shut my eyes tight. "¡Nunca cierres los ojos, Prieta!" she barked at me.

"¿Quieres que te den un chingazo en la cara?"

I shook my head, my braid swinging against my back. No chingazos for my face. She went back to her position, her hands open on either side of her face. I was ready this time: my eyes open, my hands in tight fists, my knees bent so I wouldn't lose my balance, ready to punch my grandma's hand. I stared at my target and led out with my left.

Pop!

The slap of my hand against hers was loud. My eyes opened wide. It hadn't hurt. And I hadn't missed! When she saw my face, she laughed. Her whole body shook. She slapped her thigh and laughed even harder. I giggled too. We laughed till we couldn't breathe anymore. The carcajadas were so hard, we both had tears in our eyes. We wiped at them, tried to keep our faces straight, and went back to punching in the late afternoon sunlight. The orangey desert glow came in through the old heavy windows and the front screen door, there just to showcase my new moves.

The murmur of the TV faded into the background, my feet creaking against the wooden floor and light punches echoing through the house. I learned how to jab and cross, aiming my punches at different hands. *Right, right, left,* I whispered. *Left, left, right.* Ita showed me where to hit someone so it would hurt the most: the soft cartilage of la nariz. She showed me how to move out of the way if someone punched me back.

But, when I saw her small fist coming at me, I closed my eyes again.

She wanted to know what I was doing. Hadn't she told me already to never shut my eyes? Otherwise . . .

Ita leaned forward to show me a small scar on her forehead. It was so faint I could hardly see it.

"How'd you get that, Ita?"

"El cabrón del Gil me dio un cabezazo. Estábamos averiguando y me abrió la frente."

I wondered why anyone, even her ex-husband Gil, would want to headbutt my Ita's forehead enough to open it up. He seemed nice, always gave me Chiclets and quarters for the candy machine whenever we saw him.

"Nunca cierres los ojos, Prieta, ¿eh? Tienes que 'star lista, porque nunca sabes de dónde va venir un chingazo."

I stared at the scar, a thin white *V* that widened toward her reddish hairline and nodded.

Looking back, not closing my eyes was the best advice Ita ever gave me. Life has had a way of throwing chingazos from the places I least expected.

We went back to fighting. We took turns, her punching my hands and me punching hers. I learned to lean into my punch and pivot on my feet to put more force behind it. I now knew to lean away in the opposite direction from the punch I'd just thrown and to bob back to avoid her punch. She jabbed with her left and swayed to the right, I moved to the left and jabbed to the right, like dancing but with our fists. By the time we were done, the last hints of dusk could be seen out the screen door. My Ita's hands were red, and mine stung.

"Entonces, si alguien te pega ¿qué vas a hacer?"

"Hit them," I punched out with my right hand and did the little jump I'd seen boxers do.

"¿No busques pleito, pero no te dejes de nadie, eh, Prieta?"

"I won't look for a fight, Ita. But I'll be ready if someone starts one."

THREE

BY ELEMENTARY SCHOOL, I was at home in a bar. I spent lots of weekends in them, sitting on barstools beside my Ita. Sometimes it was for fun, and sometimes it was because Ita had to trabajar on her jewelry raffles. She often bought gold jewelry at pawn shops and had her own makeshift raffles for extra money. We went to the bars she frequented and sold numbers for three or four dollars. On these days, she'd order tonic water and talk to lots of people.

"Comprarme un número," she'd smile, holding out a folded piece of paper with a list of numbers.

And people bought her numbers. What were a few dollars after a couple drinks?

But today was for fun and The Tap, my favorite bar, was like a second home to me. I knew how to maneuver us to empty seats in a crowd and to stay away from the beer pulls where we'd be lost to the bartenders and in the waitresses' way. My favorite thing to do was to spin around on the plush barstools while I stared at the floor with my dangling feet stretching toward the metal footrest.

There was something glamorous about The Tap. It looked like a bar I'd seen in a Rock Hudson movie: tables with black retro rolling chairs lining the mirrored wall, the mirrors with red neon piping along their edges, low lighting, a long narrow bar, the whole place permeated by the smell of stale cigarette smoke, of last night's shots and beer, and Frank Sinatra playing in the background. Only instead of Frank, Vicente Fernández—one of the biggest Mexican singers, king of thc rancheras, Chente with his mariachi hat, thick bushy brows, and mustache—was god here, and the bar sang along to *his* songs, not Frank's.

This Saturday was fight night: Tyson vs. Ferguson. Everyone, including my grandma, was bouncier and gave off an energy that had me wiggling in my stool. They talked louder, drank faster, and filled already-full ashtrays to overflowing. We sat at the bar, a virgin Bloody Mary in front of me and a vodka tonic in front of her. We stared at the large TV in the corner and watched as men spoke the favored odds. I didn't understand odds, but I cheered for Tyson because my grandma did. I preferred to look at the box suspended from the center of the ceiling behind the bar which held a 3-D replica of the Budweiser Clydesdales all in gold and lights.

Years of my grandma working at a bar and being a general social fixture meant we weren't alone for long.

Many nights, I sat and listened to my grandma gossiping with her close friend, comadre Veronica—"Vaca" to me, "India" to my grandma.

My mom told me the story—many times!—of when they first met. At the time, Ita had been a bartender at the D'Carlo, another bar in central El Paso, and Vaca had been a waitress on the restaurant side. Ita had taken Vaca under her wing after she saw the waitress crying at the bar one night. Vaca was brokenhearted, short on money, and drinking her sorrows away.

"¡Qué pendejadas son esas! No, señorita, no sea pendeja, amárrese un huevo, que nadie nunca la vea emborrachándose y llorando, menos por un hombre. Los viejos no valen la pena. ¿En dónde está su orgullo de mujer? Usted tiene que hacerse valer como mujer, como mujer que es, aunque se la esté llevando la chingada."

Ita believed a woman should never—ever—cry over a man, much less in a bar. It was time for Vaca to woman up and get over it.

Maybe the talk had stuck? Because looking at Vaca years later, I couldn't imagine her crying. I heard her joke around with men who were too drunk. They said things that made me look down and pretend not to hear. She always came back with something quick, put them in their place, but kept them ordering—of course.

I sat back into the plush cushion as Ita talked with Vaca for a minute. We always sat in her bar section. Then Vaca laughed her throaty laugh and walked toward outstretched hands waving for beer.

Ita asked, "¿Tienes hambre ya, Prieta?"

"No, Ita. I'm fine," I said, shaking my head.

"Bueno, nomás dime y te ordenamos una hamburger con fries."

I nodded as someone my grandma knew came up to her right at that moment. I could barely hear what he was saying because he kept leaning in toward Ita's face. I saw her shaking her head. Her gold arracadas exaggerated her movements. She laughed and patted him on the shoulder. She knew so many people—sometimes they all seemed the same. I remembered this man because he had a mustache that hung around his mouth, and his hair was salt and pepper on the sides. When he talked, I'd stare at the hair above his lips twitching back and forth like a rat. She never spoke to him for long.

"Mira, ¿te acuerdas de mi Prieta?" My grandma turned toward me and patted my leg.

"Hi!" I said, with a tiny wave, trying to sink into the back of the stool. I didn't want to shake Mustache Man's hand.

He thought I was Ita's youngest daughter.

My grandma laughed. People always thought I was her daughter. It meant all the Avon and Estée Lauder my mom bought her was paying off. We didn't look anything alike, but still she loved it. And I loved my grandma, so I always had a big grin when this happened. When Angie, my older sister, was my age, everyone really thought she was Ita's daughter because she looked exactly like Ita with her fair skin and arched brows.

"No." She shook her head, her arracadas swaying. "Es mi nieta. La traigo conmigo pa árriba y pa ábajo cuando está trabajando mi hija."

"Pa árriba y pa ábajo" is border Spanish. Ita always said this—we went up and down. It seemed like we were always walking up and down around hilly central El Paso when Ita took care of me.

When Mustache Man asked where Mom worked, Ita tilted her head back just a little, showing off. She loved to tell people about my mom's job. Ita explained how Mom worked long hours with Customs but how she helped Mom so much. I wish my mom could see how proud Ita was of her, but Mom was always at work.

"Y yo cuido a la chavala." She patted my lap again.

"La chavala" was another nickname Ita had for me. In English, "the girl" sounds so unaffectionate. It's not the same. Maybe she called me that because I was the youngest one in the family.

Mustache Man and Ita kept talking. I turned my stool away from them and pretended I was watching the fights before the main event.

I took a sip of my Bloody Mary and let the peppery tomato sit in my mouth before I swallowed. I'd tried Shirley Temples because I liked her movies, but I hadn't liked her drink. I'd even sneaked a sip of my grandma's vodka tonics, but I *really* didn't like her drinks, so I stuck to Bloody Marys. Sometimes if I drank them too fast, Ita looked at me with her eyes stern, and I knew I would have to wait a while before I had another.

We watched the fight for a while without talking. I booed when my grandma did and yelled, "¡Pégale! ¡Pégale!" when she did. During the fourth round, I told my grandma I was hungry. She ordered the hamburger and papitas she'd promised earlier. I dipped my fries into the chile that came with my burger, making sure each one was coated before I bit in.

The volume of the TV was all the way up. The crowd roared. The announcers yelled louder to be heard. Everyone in the bar screamed and laughed. Vaca maneuvered back and forth across the bar handing drink after drink to what I could only make out as groups of hands. Waitresses carried plates high above their heads, bobbing and weaving between the people too busy staring at the screen. It was a well-choreographed dance.

I sat, my legs crossed ankle to ankle on my stool and scooted closer to my grandma. I ate slowly, watching the people around me. In the fifth round, the bar became one loud fist of noise. Everyone yelled out at the same time, then the voices lulled into a low rumble. I saw Ferguson's face bloodied. My grandma held her left arm out and said, "Ya se acabó este pedo."

"Why is it over? What happened, Ita?"

"His nose is broken. Después de eso no tiene sentido, Prieta."

"Oh," I nodded as if I understood. The fight was stopped the next round. I pretended like I knew it was going to happen. I bobbed my head up and down with everyone else.

After the fight, many people left, but we stayed with a group of other regulars. I'd already had too many Bloody Marys and switched to Coke. Today Ita didn't seem to mind how many I was drinking. My grandma kept to her vodka tonics and her friends. One of the regular guitar players walked around now, and my grandma sang a few of her favorite songs.

(Search for Amalia Mendoza's "Amarga Navidad" and listen while you read.)

"Diciembre me gustó pa' que te vayas, que sea tu cruel adiós," she sang with her eyes closed. As she gained momentum, she turned to look at me.

Ita loved to sing. I think that was one of the ways she hoped people would remember her. She told me a story once that when she was a teen, a music promoter had seen her singing somewhere. She used to sing while her dad played guitar. The man had approached her and Mamá Lupe, my great grandma, about a career as a singer in Mexico. Mamá Lupe quickly said no. Ita didn't open her mouth. She never told me where her dad stood in this story.

"Why didn't you say anything, Ita?" I'd asked.

"Tenía miedo, Prieta. ¿Y si fuera una mentira? Era una chavala."

I couldn't imagine Ita scared.

"But what if it wasn't a lie?"

She'd just shrugged.

Ita continued to sing. I stared back at her thinking of that story, quiet, not knowing what to do, but the magic of her voice wrapped me in its lonely blanket. *"Mi navidad no quiero comenzar el año nuevo, con este mismo amor, que me hace tanto mal."*

The small audience around us began to disperse. Then it was just us. Her voice seemed to express everything she could never say in words. In these moments, my chest tightened, and I imagined what I'd be like later. Would I be like Ita, a huge wall of tough exterior protecting her from whatever made her eyes shine when she sang? She patted my knee and turned back toward the bar.

That day, I stood on the rung of the chair and hugged her around the waist when she sat down. I pushed my face into her polyester shirt, which smelled like gardenia and smoke. I squeezed my eyes tight as I clutched her.

"¿Qué te pasa, Prieta? No más es una canción. ¿Qué te pusieron en los Bloody Marys?" she asked, laughing.

She pulled on my braid to look at my face. I looked up into her brown, cat-lined eyes and grimaced at her joke about me having too many drinks. I didn't usually cry when she sang, but this song had sounded different.

Heavier. Sadder.

"I don't like that song, Ita," I said, still looking at her eyes, which held only half the laughter.

She told me she wouldn't sing it anymore, but I knew it wasn't true.

"¿Quieres poner música?"

I nodded as she reached for her purse, a beige tote with worn straps where she could find anything. She gave me quarters for the jukebox. The crowd thinned since it was late. I made my way between the people standing in front of the jukebox. I paged through the artists even though I knew what songs I'd pick: "Llorar y Llorar" by Chente and "Payaso" by Javier Solís. I looked over. Ita was watching me even while she was talking to Víctor, the owner of The Who's, another bar close by. From where I stood, I saw the way her feet hung from the rung by the thin heel of her metallic strappy sandals. When she laughed, she threw her head back, her face scrunched, her whole body moving, her chest and stomach trembling.

I walked back to Ita, following the gentle slope of the bar's floor. A group of men sat at a table near the jukebox and pointed at me as I walked by. One of them said, "¡Mira, una mascota en la barra!" They all laughed. I pretended I didn't hear them. Chente had just started to play when I saw Ita paying the tab.

"Ya nos vamos, Prieta. Te doy más cambio en el Who's."

The Who's was my second favorite bar after The Tap. We said bye to Vaca, who blew me a kiss. She was busy with people trying to squeeze in one last round. My grandma wrapped the straps from her purse around the wrist of her left hand and held my hand with her right. We walked out and made our way to her boat-like 1968 Buick Rivera.

It was warm out. I rolled down the window as she walked around to the driver's side. The night was quiet except for the music escaping through The Tap's door, opening and closing as people walked out. There was a man on the corner curled up in a sleeping bag. His pillow looked like a bag of junk. I turned away when I saw his eyes weren't closed.

The Who's was just a couple blocks away from The Tap on Mesa Street, but we always drove because it was so late at night. When we got there, the place was only half full and getting ready to close. The boss, Víctor, was already at a table across from the small rectangular dance floor and the jukebox. We sat and said hi to all the people there. I couldn't remember all of their names—"Pájaro," "La Borada,"—but her friend Suzi, called "Flaca," was there and another one of her comadres, Elsie, was behind the bar closing down.

We'd stayed after hours at The Who's several times before. Only a select few stayed. We were like the VIPs when the lights dimmed and we moved to a table in the back. My grandma's inner circle sat around a table littered with ash, glasses of multicolored drinks, and brown beer bottles. One of the musicians stayed, but by this time he'd joined in on the drinks. All the regular people left. I got to put money in the jukebox, which I liked because The Who's jukebox had songs we could dance to. I put on Chente again and Javier Solís, but this time I also picked Glenn Miller's "In the Mood" and "The Charleston."

(Both wonderful songs. You should listen to them while you read.)

I drank my Coke and pulled out the extra cherries that Elsie had put in it for me. But when "In the Mood" came on, Ita smiled at me and said, "¡Vente, Prieta!"

We danced around the small floor. My tennis shoes squeaked and stuck, while my grandma sashayed in her heels, leading me by one arm. She kicked out and in. I tried my best to imitate her. Her friends at the table whistled and clapped for us when the song was finally over. My stomach hurt from laughing and dancing.

Víctor laughed and yelled out, "¡Lichita, la chavala es tu sombra!" Everyone else nodded and chuckled.

In many ways, I am my Ita's sombra. How could I not be like her?

We bowed when we finished—arms swinging up big and out, first to each other, then to her friends. Jutting her chin up, she pushed her reddish hair back as if she were a serious dancer, her arracadas danced. We were both out of breath.

By this time, it was way after two. Each of her friends chose songs they knew so they could sing along and talk in between. I put my head on my grandma's lap. She ran her nails through the unbraided part of my hair, close to the scalp.

"¿Tiene sueño la chavala?" Víctor asked.

Grandma's body rocked as she nodded. A few minutes later, she shook my shoulder before I completely fell asleep, her hand warm on my skin. Víctor lifted me, placing my body on top of the bar.

"Aquí tienes tu almohada y tu cobija, Prieta," my grandma said as she covered me. "Ya es tarde, duérmete."

I felt cared for. The pillow and blanket were just part of it. I was a child in an adult world and got all the attention. What more could I ask for?

I curled up, my knees tucked up into my stomach, and stared as the dim lights overhead reflected on the bottles along the wall.

Tomorrow was Sunday. My mom would pick me up. I knew I'd be able to sleep because she'd be tired from working through the night. She'd sleep most of the day and then we'd order in. I thought about suggesting pizza as I snuggled deeper into the blanket and felt the coolness of the wooden bar warm from my body.

Víctor turned down the volume of the jukebox. It fell to a low background noise, barely louder than everyone's voices. Green, brown, and red glimmers of light reflected off the mirror behind them, lulling me to sleep as they danced and twinkled their way into my dreams.

FOUR

AFTER A WEEK of tears, Mrs. Mahoney, my first-grade teacher, called the principal.

"I don't know why she's crying," my grandma told the teacher, speaking in her slightly accented English.

Mrs. Mahoney and Mr. Taylor stared down at me. I tried to disappear behind my grandma's leg. I hoped she'd stay, but she'd already begun to back away from my embrace as she had every other morning at drop off. The warm fleece fabric of her sweatpants pulled from my clammy hands. Snot ran from my nose, onto my lip, and into my mouth, mingling with the briny taste of tears. Mr. Taylor looked down into my face and asked in his raspy voice, "Don't you want to be with your friends? Look, they're all looking at you, and no one's crying about coming to school."

I scanned the kids seated in my class and shook my head. The burn got hotter on my cheeks, like when I stood too close to the stove helping my Ita cook. I looked down at my scuffed pink Converse and away from Mr. Taylor's big white face that smelled of ashtrays. I stared at the door. He'd made my grandma leave. I didn't care that the other kids weren't crying. All I knew was that I didn't want to be here, away from my mom, my grandma, and my sister.

I turned and shuffled toward my desk. I gulped puffs of air, my chest heaving forward in small bursts, and slumped down in my seat. The principal kept talking to Mrs. Mahoney, who stared back at me. I pretended not to listen, tracing the name Jose, scratched on the right-hand corner of my desk, over and over. The other kids turned in my direction, their faces wrinkled, mouths open, the boys trying not to giggle too loud.

My kindergarten teacher, Mrs. Worman, was warm and smelled of cinnamon. Her classroom walls were cluttered with brightly colored cutouts, posters telling us to read, and green pouch-like felt smiley faces with our names on them. These held small Legos that tracked our good behavior for a prize at week's end. I'd always gotten a prize, like a sheet of shiny stickers.

Mrs. Mahoney's room was not like that. Only a few green and yellow posters with Lamar Longhorn, our school mascot, were tacked on the otherwise empty walls. The windows showed the row of houses and buildings carved into the downward slope of the Franklin mountains. The room was bare and cold. The bright fluorescent lights made all our brown faces look yellow, like at the doctor's office.

Why couldn't I just stay with Mrs. Worman?

Mrs. Mahoney gave me hard, unblinking glares that reminded me of my great-grandma Mamá Lupe, but worse because Mrs. Mahoney didn't wear glasses. She walked around the room and slammed her ruler on our desks if she thought we weren't paying attention. *If she hits my desk, she's going to hit my hand,* I thought. I peered at a few of the other kids who'd been in Mrs. Worman's class and wondered why they liked this new teacher with a face like when I sneaked drinks from my grandma's dark black coffee.

I wiped the boogers that ran from my nose onto my arm, afraid to ask for a Kleenex. If I made myself small after what I'd just done—cried so much she'd called the principal—maybe I'd disappear. *Small, be small,* I thought as I imagined shrinking into myself, until I was a tiny little ball that could roll away, out the door, through the front entrance of the school, down Circle Drive's slope until it hit California Avenue. Then I'd be in Ita's living room watching *General Hospital* or *All My Children* with her.

But then I gulped. The noise bounced off the blank white walls, echoed between their many empty spots, each gulp making me big like air being blown into a balloon. Too bad there wasn't enough air in me so I could blow up and float out of the school. I would wave goodbye to ugly Mrs. Mahoney and glide up the nearby mountains, never to return to her classroom.

Every morning the crying started again, until finally everyone had had enough. My mom came straight from a graveyard shift at the Paso del Norte International Bridge, one of three bridges that connected us to Juárez, to talk to Mr. Taylor. It was 8:30 a.m. We sat in his office, across from his oversized wooden desk, my mom in her navy-blue Customs uniform, my legs sticking straight out of his big green chairs like two brown matchsticks. His office smelled like The Tap.

I'd never been in it before. Only really bad kids came here.

I didn't feel like a bad kid—I never hit anyone or anything like that—but I still shrunk into the chair. I did notice that the principal's face wasn't as wrinkled when he spoke to Mom as when he looked at me, and his eyes didn't dart back and forth to the door like he was wishing she would leave right away. Or he could get out.

"Mrs. Ramirez, we don't know what to do any more. Has anything happened at home that would explain the morning tears? We've had other children who didn't want to come to school, but after a week they liked coming." His voice rumbled from deep in his chest, bounced off the inside of him like a ball in a pinball machine before it escaped out of his mouth.

"Well, to be honest, Mr. Taylor," my mother said, "she doesn't like her teacher, Mrs. Mahoney. You know, I work a lot, my mom brings her to school every day because of that, and I think it would help if she liked the class she was in. She needs to like where she's going, to feel comfortable. Don't you think?"

He cleared his throat, swallowing one of the pinballs.

"All our teachers are great, Mrs. Ramirez. I don't understand the issue, but if you think it would help—"

"I do. Yes." She smiled big, only it didn't reach her eyes.

The words hung heavy in the air. When my mom smiled like that, I knew she wasn't really smiling. The air around her stiffened. I scooted farther back in my chair.

"Is there a teacher you had in mind, Mrs. Ramirez?"

"Can I be in Karen's class, Mom?" I said real quick, turning my face up to her, ignoring the thick staticky air.

"Now, we can't just move her into another class because

she wants to be with one of her friends, Mrs. Ramirez," he said, his words rushing out in one garbled breath.

"I understand, Mr. Taylor, but *I think* all my daughter needs is something familiar. You yourself said, 'Most children would have adjusted by now.' Yasmín needs something a little familiar. I don't think that's asking too much."

Mr. Taylor shuffled some papers on his desk and cleared his throat. I made a small steeple against the wood of his desk with the tips of my white and pink Converse.

He stopped shuffling papers and inhaled. His breath sounded like an air conditioner vent vibrating against the wall.

"Mrs. Ramirez, I printed the class rosters for the first-grade teachers, and all the classes are full. Mrs. John's class is the only one that isn't. I believe that *Yaz-mine* will feel more comfortable in that class. It's not the one with her friend, you understand, because that class is already full, but Mrs. John is a great teacher."

My mom shifted forward in her seat, small. When she started to get angry or annoyed, it radiated from her, like the electric heater we used in the bathroom when we took baths at my Ita's house.

"Mom, Mrs. John sounds fine."

I reached out to put my hand on her lap but changed my mind and left it hanging in the air.

"Are you sure?"

"Yeah, Mom . . ."

As she turned toward Mr. Taylor, I let my hand fall on the top of her blue thigh. The material was thick and stiff, but the touch of her hand on mine was soft and warm.

From that day on, I was no longer in Mrs. Mahoney's class. I walked into her classroom to get my pencil box and the emergency sweater I kept in my cubbyhole, avoiding her gaze and the odd looks I received from the other kids. My mom stood in the doorway, waiting for me.

"After this," she said, "there can't be any more crying, okay? They aren't going to keep changing your classes. You have to come to school like all the other kids." The soles of her heavy work boots echoed in the long hallway.

I nodded, my braid bobbing against my back.

I said goodbye to her at the door of Mrs. John's class. Strands of her hair surrounded her head in a messy halo. Her eyes were red, her shoulders sagged a little. She'd just finished a midnight to eight a.m. shift and had to go back at four. But she had still come to school with me.

"Ready?" she asked me.

"Yeah, Mom." I wrapped my arms around her, the leather of her belt digging into the side of my head. I gripped her pants, but the thick uniform material slipped out of my hands. She smoothed my hair back. Time for me to let go. She waited as I adjusted my backpack on my shoulders.

"Do you want me to wait?"

"No, Mom, it's okay."

As I walked into the new class, I turned to see her hovering just outside the doorway. In her dark uniform, with her handcuffs and backup ammo hanging from her hips, my petite mom seemed even smaller. She'd left her nightstick and gun in the car. I didn't know how to tell the people at school that I also cried before my mom went to work and clung to her rigid uniform pants as she left. I cried when she walked away from me, nightstick swaying, so scared I said the same prayer over and over to Diosito: "Please don't let my mom die. Please don't let her die."

I watched the local news with my Ita when Estela Casas reported on Customs agents who'd made a large drug bust on one of the bridges from Juárez. The news showed two officers holding football-sized shrink-wrapped bundles. Ita prayed out loud, "Ay, Diosito, cuida a mi Gorda, que no le pase nada, y que nadie le haga daño." She rubbed her hands in a circle like she was wrapping my mother with her love and prayers.

I wondered: could Diosito put a force field around my mom if I prayed hard enough like Ita to protect her? I studied the two officers on the television. They had black leather belts like my mom's, silver revolvers, and the same nightsticks, except theirs were bigger. They were men.

When I cried, everyone—the teachers, Ita, and my mom—asked what was wrong. My sister tried to make me feel better, but after a while she thought I was just being bratty. I didn't know how to tell anyone what I was afraid of, so I just cried until the tears dried on my face and my head ached. Sometimes my mouth tried to form the words: *because you could die.*

But I never told anyone. If I did, it might happen. The words stayed anchored in the back of my throat, just like I hoped the bullets would stay secure in her holster.

FIVE

SUNDAY, ITA AND I woke up early to go to church, even though mass didn't begin until noon. She never let me eat beforehand because she believed it was better to take the hostia on an empty stomach. So I sat in the center of her bed and watched as she slathered creams, lotions, and perfumes on, trying to convince myself I wasn't hungry. My stomach gurgled.

The radio on the nightstand played a fuzzy "Amor Eterno" by Rocío Dúrcal.

(Search for Rocío Dúrcal's "Amor Eterno" and listen while you read. It's beautiful.)

The song, written by Juan Gabriel, a Mexican singer and icon who just happened to be from Juárez, was about the death and eternal love of his mother.

Ita ironed her pants and blouse and laid them out on the bed. I shifted over, careful not to disturb her outfit. Ita hated wrinkles and getting dirty. She got ready for the day the same way she got ready for bed, only in reverse. On Sundays, she took longer than usual. I couldn't decide if she was getting dressed up for God or for Mamá Lupe: they both seemed to make her pray more.

The mixed floral scent of Skin So Soft bath oil perfumed the room. She smeared thick Avon sunscreen on her fair face, then put on eye shadow, black liquid eyeliner, and mascara. Her dyed reddish-brown hair was wrapped around small metal rollers she'd slept with and wore until she dressed. She did her hair last. She didn't want it to go flat.

The early morning breeze kept us fresh. It came in through the heavy framed window in her bedroom. She kept it propped open with a broken wooden broom handle. In the summer, desert mornings are always cool, but the morning dew quickly evaporates the higher the sizzling sun rises. The fan on her chest of drawers rotated back and forth, shaking its trembling body against the heat's arrival.

Ita sang along to "Amor Eterno" as she put on her pantyhose. I lay quiet on my side, listening. I propped my head in my hand, dangling my feet in my pink and purple high-tops off the side of the bed. Ita sang, reached for her bra and adjusted the weight of the silicone in the right cup, making sure it was even. She leaned over as she put it on, letting herself fall into it. "*Me miro en el espejo y veo en mi rostro. El tiempo que he sufrido por tu adiós.*"

She stood in front of the mirror, adjusting, always careful that the scar on her chest, a reminder of the fight she'd won against breast cancer, didn't peek out from the top of the bra, and that the line of her bust was even.

She turned, elbows bent, palms open, fingers curled, grasping at the air, and sang directly to me when the song reached the chorus where the singer wished her mother was still alive. Ita stretched her arm out toward me with an exaggerated vibrato in her voice and movement in her lips on the last word until I started giggling. She kissed her hand, waved to the invisible audience in the room, and erupted into laughter.

"¿Qué piensas, Prieta?" she asked, arched brows pulsing up and down.

She stopped quickly and turned back toward the mirror, assessing herself: her pantyhose pulled high up on her waist, almost meeting the bra line, pointed beige lace bra hiding the scar on her body, and her face, eyes cat-lined, smooth skin glistening. Her age only showed in the small stamps of laughter left around her eyes and mouth and the subtle softening of her skin. Though laughter had gleamed in her eyes moments earlier, now she was critical, gazing so hard at her reflection, it made me turn away.

By eleven o'clock we were ready to go. She looked at herself one last time, dabbed pink lipstick on her lips, and made a kissy face so the shade was even.

We locked the heavy wooden door and let the screen door slam, *clank, clank,* behind us. I hopped down the twenty-five concrete stairs to her large gray 1968 Buick Riviera, which she always warmed up for at least fifteen minutes before any drive, no matter what season. We sat with the windows rolled down, but inside the air was close and searing.

The sun streamed in through the windshield and made us squint against the light. Tiny drops of sweat sprung to the surface on the skin above my lip and across the bridge of my nose. The seats of the car itched against my legs, the fabric stiff and powdery with age. The car's overhead lining sagged in places. I had to pull the seat belt slowly, so it would fit me the way it was supposed to. Ita pulled on a flowery cover she'd cut from a long-sleeved blouse to protect her left arm against the sun's blistering rays. But even with the heat, sweat now bubbling at my hairline, we sat waiting for the stuffy air to escape and the car to warm up.

She fiddled with the dial on the radio, trying to find one of the three Spanish stations it played. The giant oak tree beside the car gave little pieces of shade. When we finally drove off, I welcomed the breeze even though it was still hot.

In the desert, unless it's nighttime, the breeze is always just a swirl of warm air.

The drive downtown to Sacred Heart church didn't take long, but we liked to arrive early to find a parking space. It took some time. We almost missed one because we had to drive around the block. As we drove, Ita said over and over, "¡Que no lo vean, Diosito! ¡Que no lo vean!" I imagined God putting an invisibility cloak around the parking spot so that others wouldn't see it. Maybe God didn't have anything better to do because a space was waiting for us.

Sagrado Corazón is nestled in the farthest east corner of downtown El Paso's Segundo Barrio. It is one of the oldest churches in El Paso. The neighborhood was one of the first in the city actually. Many of the buildings in the area, like the church, were built in the late 1800s. I think that's why we went there. There was a closer and fancier church—St. Patrick's—by Ita's house, but we still drove downtown to come to this one. Everything we did was always downtown.

We hurried to walk the two blocks to Sagrado Corazón, me in my high-top sneakers and my grandma in her high nude wedges. Her pink polyester pants had a thin seam down the center, and her floral top made me think of spring. She looked so pretty just to go to church.

When we entered, Ita searched for my great-grandmother, Mamá Lupe. I sighed with the freshness inside the church as sweat trickled down the small of my back. We stopped at the beginning of the red-carpeted aisle. I dipped my fingers into the large ivory holy water font and let them linger in the cool water. I crossed myself, top, bottom, left, right. I bowed down in a small curtsy and crossed myself again, then walked down the long aisle separating the pews.

I didn't like coming to church, having to sit still on the hard wooden pews for an hour as the priest spoke. It made me fidgety. I *really* didn't like it when we had to shake hands toward the end of the mass—I didn't like touching strangers' clammy hands. And the part I disliked the most was sitting with Mamá Lupe and her husband Pablo. She smelled like stale cigarettes and mothballs. Each time she stared at me through her thick glasses, I wanted to look down, away, at anything but her lined face. But I came almost every Sunday with my Ita because my mom worked so much, and this was the one time a week my grandma saw Mamá Lupe. I knew it was important to her because she took so much longer getting ready than usual, ironing her clothes, lining her eyes. I didn't understand why. She was always quiet when we left, the car ride home silent as I played with my seat belt and stared out the window.

¡

I learned later that Mamá Lupe was just unhappy and made others feel the same way whenever she had the chance. There were stories: Mamá Lupe's parents had left her; her grandparents raised her; Ita's dad had left Mamá Lupe and their four children for another woman; Ita was her dad's favorite—he played the guitar for her when she was young, and that's why Mamá Lupe was harder on her . . . the theories went on.

The only thing I knew was the way my grandma seemed after she saw her mother, like a wilted flower that didn't have enough water.

The cool quiet church made me feel a little more at ease. My breathing slowed, but my hands stayed sweaty. I rubbed them on my shorts, again and again. Ita found Mamá Lupe's short crop of gray hair among the other heads staring at the pulpit and scooted down her row past the people who were already sitting. When we got to Mamá Lupe, I leaned in and kissed the thin, wrinkled skin on her cheek, avoiding the hard gaze she gave me through her large nude-colored plastic glasses.

"Hola, Mamá Lupe," I mumbled. "Hola, Pablo." I waved at her husband.

I sat to the right of my grandma, so I wouldn't have to sit next to them.

I stared at the white-robed priest in front of the church and half-listened to his mass. It was in Spanish, and sometimes he used really formal words I didn't know. I studied the great hall of the church and all the statues in their alcoves. I stared at the stained-glass windows and tried to understand the story depicted in the red, green, and white shards of glass put together so delicately. The sun streamed in, but the stories diluted its heat. Diosito stood at the front, arms splayed to his sides, his gaze upward, eyes wide, defeated. I looked up and felt the same way. My stomach growled.

Toward the end of the mass, we stood in line and waited our turn as the priest served communion. My palms got damper the closer we got. I never knew whether to hold my hands up or to stick my tongue out. I thought that if I stuck my tongue out, the hostia would somehow be purer, but I didn't want the priest to look in my mouth or touch my tongue. I stood next in line and held my sweaty cupped hands out as the priest said, "Cuerpo de Cristo." I walked away and let the small white circle sit on my tongue till it disintegrated.

Why did God taste like paper?

After church, we went to eat at the Acapulco, a small nearby diner with a jukebox in the corner that always played "All My Ex's Live in Texas." By the time we arrived, my stomach was in a knot. God had done nothing to subdue my hunger. I put extra salsa in my soup and then ate my caldo de res. The spice overtook the heat of the broth so that it stung my lips with each slurp. I liked the sting of the soup that was brimful with carrots, celery, zucchini, beef chunks, and rice. When I fished out the meat chunks and dropped them into a corn tortilla, I added more salsa on top of the taco. The soup was like two meals in one.

Mamá Lupe and my grandma did all the talking. Pablo rarely spoke on any occasion. I always worried that he'd choose this lunch after church to speak to me, but he didn't. I was invisible, and I didn't mind. This was the perk of being a kid. Ita patted my leg every so often. I didn't have anything to say to Mamá Lupe, and I don't think she had anything to say to me.

When I did try to say something, she lectured me about speaking English instead of Spanish because Pablo, who was from Juárez, didn't understand it. Or on the correct way to address her—"usted instead of tú," the first being more respectful—but then I would get my word conjugations all mixed up. When she asked me how my mom was, I took longer chewing so my grandma had to answer for me. The next time she asked me something, I pretended to forget the words in Spanish. She gave up talking to me, which suited me just fine.

Mamá Lupe and Ita's conversation slid into the background as I listened to the jukebox and stared at the waitress with the large red bouffant who alternated between taking orders and talking to the hairnetted cook in the kitchen.

After each lunch, Ita and I left with goodbyes and dry kisses on their wrinkled cheeks. We walked to our car, the only sound our shoes against the pavement. Ita always grew quiet after Mamá Lupe's "Adios, *Alicia*," said in a tone I didn't understand, that made me feel as if I'd done something wrong.

Years later, when I was in middle school, Mamá Lupe died. My grandma was the only one of her four children living in

El Paso. She'd had a stroke while waiting in the car for Pablo to buy some milk. Instead of taking her to the hospital, he drove home and called my grandma. My grandma sat by her bedside, holding her hand and talking, hoping she'd wake up. Before her siblings arrived, Ita whispered, "I'm here. The daughter you never loved."

"Mamá, aquí estoy, la hija que nunca quisiste."

Mamá Lupe hadn't opened her eyes, but tears had escaped. We believe that although she couldn't speak, she still knew Ita was there, knew she was the only one who had truly ever been there. Mamá Lupe never regained her mobility or her ability to speak. She died a few days later in the hospital. She was eighty-five. My grandma cried for days. By that time, I was eleven. Even though I didn't feel as sad, I understood Ita was. The house was quieter, still. Her volume had been turned down. Ita was always bigger than life but now I saw her shrink. She became small, almost frail. I was afraid she'd break.

"¿Qué quieres hacer, Prieta? ¿A la casa?" Ita asked after we left the Acapulco.

"Home? Mom's coming to get me today, isn't she? After work?"

"Sí, pero hasta más tarde. ¿Quieres una banana split? Vamos a Thirty-one Flavors?"

I never refused a visit to Baskin-Robbins.

"Sí, Ita, sí. ¡Una banana split!"

She turned the volume down on the radio when we got to the car. We drove without saying much. I always felt relieved when it was just the two of us again. I looked out the open window as we left a now near-empty downtown and headed toward Baskin-Robbins in the Five Points area. I stared at the empty streets and let the warm breeze muss the stray hair from my braid.

We walked in. I could almost taste the frosty ice-cream-scented air. We ordered and sat in the empty ice cream parlor. The heat had begun to let up a little, but the sunlight still streamed in through the windows. We were in our own snow globe, just the two of us, sitting inside the glass walls, eating our banana splits.

"Is your banana split good, Ita?" I asked, my mouth sticky from the vanilla ice cream.

"Yes, Prieta."

She took a big spoon of ice cream in her mouth and opened her mouth wide, a gooey mess of chocolate sauce and ice cream.

"Mmmm!"

"Ita!" I laughed at her, opening my mouth, but some of the ice cream dribbled out.

She laughed at me. "Okay, ya, ya. Te vas a ensuciar." She pushed a napkin toward me.

We got home just in time for my mom to pick me up. She honked, and I ran down the stairs. They both watched, my grandma in her pink pants and floral shirt standing on the porch, and my mom in her navy-blue uniform, duty belt, and aviator sunglasses looking up from her brown Blazer. My grandma waved as we drove off. She looked like a small pink flower, petals waving in the breeze.

SIX

FOR MY GRANDMA'S "third" fifty-fourth birthday (she refused to be sixty), her ex-husband Gil took us out to celebrate.

Gil and Ita had been separated as long as I could remember, but they remained friends. In fact, my grandma remained friends with some of the other men she'd married. She was a brightness that they couldn't stay far away from. But, like any other light, she sometimes shone too bright.

Ita paired a beautiful pink angora sweater with black pants and small black wedges for her birthday outfit. I wiggled around our bed as she got ready and skipped down the stairs when we left the house. For the celebration, Gil was taking us to dinner at a well-known seafood restaurant in Juárez, the Villa Del Mar, which my grandma loved. We drove down to the Bridge of the Americas and parked her big Buick in a nearby parking lot. It was a quick five-minute walk to the arched bridge over to Juárez. We took a taxi the rest of the way to meet Gil in front of the restaurant.

Gil was my grandma's fifth husband legally, seventh really. There were some common-law ones squished in there, but Ita still said they were married. At the time, I didn't know why Gil and Ita had gotten a divorce.

He stood waiting for us, looking stylish in black pants, a black jacket with a white button-down, and wayfarer sunglasses, his black hair always combed into a pompadour. He looked the same as he did in the pictures taken when they were younger except now his smooth face was pockmarked and bumpy. My grandma waved as we got close. He walked over to us with a big smile, said he wanted to take my grandma to a tienda next door first.

Downtown Juárez was haphazardly dynamic. The busy, sometimes narrow, streets were filled with cars, taxi drivers, and big buses letting out puffs of gray smoke and crammed with too many people. There were retail stores next to fancy restaurants next to dive taquerías, and a bar that played mariachi music so loud, anyone could hear it on the street even at ten in the morning. In movies, Juárez is always shown with dirt roads and random homeless donkeys walking around, but the only donkey I ever saw was in the tourist area. It was right in front of the Mexico side of the bridge. Brown-faced men who wore sombreros and sarapes—even in the summer heat—overcharged gringos to pose on top of or next to the donkey for a Polaroid picture. I asked my grandma once if I could take a picture too.

She shook her head, "No, señorita. Eso es para los gringos pendejos."

I nodded as if I understood. Silly gringos?

Now we stood in front of the store, the noisy cars and gassy scent of exhaust around us. My grandma didn't want to visit the store at first but gave in because Gil's face was all smiles. Since the morning, we'd been bouncy singing and wiggling to the music playing from her old staticky radio. When we caught our first glance of the window, I realized why he wanted to take my grandma there. She was so busy talking, she almost didn't notice, but when she saw them, she let out a tiny gasp.

There they were: pink sling-back marabou heels, sitting on a metal display pedestal, waiting for her. Gil threw his head back, let out a big laugh, a carcajada, and clapped his hands together.

"¿Qué te dije, mamita?"

He knew she would love them instantly. We walked in, then walked right out with the shoes in my grandma's tiny size five. When we got to the restaurant, we laughed, and Gil told jokes that had us laughing even louder. We started with calamari appetizers and salads. Each time the waiter came back, Gil ordered a Dos Equis.

When it was time for us to order our food, he insisted we order the most expensive things, like the lobster. I glanced at my grandma to make sure it was okay. She ordered for me instead, even though Gil protested, gesturing with the beer in his hand. By the time our food came, I was so caught up in the laughter, I hadn't realized my grandma wasn't laughing as loudly. The next time the waiter came by, Gil asked for another beer.

"Cálmate, ¿no? Todavía es temprano." She rolled her eyes toward me as I pretended not to notice, staring at my pink shrimp.

It was still early, just like she said, but Ita already knew where this was headed. He didn't seem to be calming down at all and instead boasted he was fine.

"Estoy bien. Estoy bien, mamita. ¡Es tu cumpleaños! ¡Debemos celebrar!" He ordered another beer.

He had gotten too loud. People stared at us. Ita no longer ate her trout, and I only stared at the large shrimp cocktail in front of me. I put my hand on my grandma's leg beneath the table, and she squeezed it tight, then let go. The bill came with the next beer even though we hadn't asked for it, and Gil chugged it down as my grandma stood.

We walked out.

Gil asked where we were going next. "¿A dónde vamos, mamita?" He threw his hand around her waist.

"Ya nos vamos a la casa. Es tarde. Gracias por la comida y los zapatos." Ita's voice had changed, stiff and hard as she thanked him for the shoes. I didn't know what was happening, but I was glad we were going home.

"¿Cómo que la 'casa'?" He pulled my grandma toward him and buried his face in her neck.

She pulled away. "¡Cálmate tu pedo, eh!" Her hand squeezed mine tighter.

"Ándale, mamita," Gil said. The laughter had left his voice.

"Ya, se acabó, Gil." She cut the air with her hand.

She was telling him it was over in more ways than one. Maybe when he drank, he forgot which parts were over. We turned and walked away as he stood on the dingy sidewalk. My grandma's wedges clicked loud, even with the city noise. I had to take faster steps to keep up. The shoe bag kept bumping against my leg. I turned once and saw him standing where we had left him. We rounded the corner and walked several more blocks, weaving in and out of people.

"Ita?"

She stopped, turned, and stared at me as if she was just realizing I was with her. She gazed down and saw the hand she clasped turning red. People moved around us, and she pulled me closer to a storefront. She smoothed her sweaty hand against her pants and turned away. I expected tears, but her eyes were dry. The look in them made me want to cry, and my throat burned, knowing that I couldn't. The hollow expression on her face, her dark eyes, her faded pink lips pursed as she looked down at me, told me it wasn't the first time Gil had gotten so drunk. Why did my grandma still try to be his friend? Why didn't he understand?

Ita flagged a taxi to take us back to the bridge. We were quiet as we walked over the concrete rainbow arch back to El Paso. We stood in the short line of people waiting their turn to declare citizenship or show their shopping bags to the navy-blue clad Customs agents. I glanced around for my mom even though I knew she wasn't working at this bridge. When it was our turn, we both mumbled, "American," and waited for the officer's okay to walk through.

"Any fruits, meats, or vegetables?" the agent asked, gesturing toward the white plastic bag still in my hand.

Ita glanced down at the bag and shook her head, "No, sir. Just shoes."

He nodded and waved us through the metal turnstile.

Silence filled the drive home except for the murmur of the Mexican radio station crackling through the old speakers. There was less traffic—El Paso was quieter than

Juárez—and I was glad. The sun was setting as we reached the house.

That night, we watched *Wheel of Fortune*. I had my head on my grandma's lap. The new shoes sat next to the door in the bag where I'd set them, the plastic handle wrinkled and stretched.

SEVEN

MOM TELLS ME, "Dr. Roman, your pediatrician, told me that you were one of the happiest babies he had ever seen in all his practice."

Her smile is bright every single time she says this. I nod. I've seen the old photos with my fat little baby cheeks round and full of smiles, so I believe her.

She always follows up with, "Everything changed when *the stuff* with your dad happened."

This is when the brightness vanishes. Light switch flicked off. I'm not sure what *stuff* she's talking about when she says this though. The later incidents, standing me up on visitation days, were when I was older. They separated when I was three. Who remembers anything from when they were three?

But maybe what happened is hidden in the folds of my memory like the yellow baby blanket my mom still has collecting dust in the back of her linen closet, because even Angie, who witnessed my parents' relationship from the beginning, and was already ten when I was born, said I changed.

Family history like this is weird. I've been told the story

about how my mom and dad separated so many times that I feel like I remember it too. I've created my own fragmented story out of their words and the old photos I've stared at countless times.

But that's not possible, is it?

We lived in a corner house on Nations in North Central El Paso. The Nations house was on the other side of the Franklins from Ita's house.

At first it was just me, my mom, Angie, and my dad. But Angie tells me that one day, my dad appeared with his two sons and a daughter from a previous marriage. I can imagine their faces, so similar to mine, standing next to him in a row from short to shorter. Without discussing things with my mom, they moved in with us.

So, we were all very cozy in this three-bedroom house. It was full of long silhouettes and dark wood. It was in this house that Angie found a small white snake in her room. I hear her yelling for my mom and running in and out of her bedroom doorway while the tiny snake slithered along the tile floor. In the shadows of my mind, my half-siblings aren't there. I don't know enough about them to fill in their details. Even though we must have looked alike, like our father, their faces float in and out of memory like ghosts.

My dad was a carpenter up until suddenly he wasn't. I know this because I have strong memories of the earthy smell of sawdust and the loud sounds of table saws buzzing in my small ears. I see his smile and laughter in his workshop. These aren't the layered memories I've created from stories

I've been told.

It's a shame that someone who knew wood, its grains and defects, didn't notice when our small family tree, a sapling, began to dry and splinter. The first dark stain in the wood seemed to be there from the very beginning. Maybe the differences in their jobs and income were easy to overlook early on, but the honeymoon stage didn't last for long.

When I talk about this time with Angie, she tells me, "I don't know if your dad was ever okay with the fact that the Nations house was just in Mom's name."

"But why was it?" I ask.

She shrugs and says, "You know Mom."

I nod.

Mom always had to be so strong, she lost all her flexibility. It has always been her way or the highway.

I was three years old when my mom was laid off as a phone operator from Southwestern Bell, her first time without a job. Somewhere around that time, she realized that my dad wasn't going to be the person she wanted him to be.

The whole family was at a Kmart, including my father and his kids. We were moving slowly toward the glass-doored exit when I saw the yellow and pink horse kiddie ride outside of the store and rushed to get on it. I pulled Angie with me.

I heard Mom ask Dad for ten dollars for gas. He said he didn't have it. Right then, my half-sister walked out of the store and handed him some change. He'd just bought her a record. He put a ten-dollar bill back into his wallet. My mom's lips squeezed together in a tight line.

Angie pulled me away from the kiddie ride. I smiled and waved toward my dad's stout figure as he left with his kids. I toddled next to Angie and Mom on the way to our car.

I'm certain there were signs before this moment, but Angie can only fill in parts of the story for me. She was thirteen. We were both just kids, but every time we talk about this particular incident when we're older, pieces shake free.

She talks to me as she drives down I-10, heading west toward the mountain's rocky open arms.

"You know, it was the first time the roles were reversed with Mom and your dad. Mom always had a better job, and this was the first time she didn't," she says.

My nose wrinkles. "He sounds like a dick. Mom's always been so strong. Why did she put up with that? I can't imagine just showing up at our house with his kids without saying anything."

My sister kept driving down the highway. "You know, I think Mom just really wanted it to work. Ita didn't believe your dad was good enough for Mom. Mom just wanted to prove Ita wrong. Your dad was a good man, I guess. They just had different priorities." She pauses for a moment. "You know Mom. She always had to prove everyone wrong."

I frown and look ahead toward the traffic.

Mom still tried to make it work after the ten-dollar incident. Angie tells me things built up until one day Mom just had enough. The house was a mess. Dad and his kids completely ignored the rules Mom came up with. When Mom tried to talk to him about it, he didn't want to hear it. Angie tells me she helped Mom pack up their stuff in black garbage bags. She remembers the boys' grimy room with the smell of their dirty clothes. My dad got home to black blobs piled in the front of the house, filled with his things and his kids' things.

I followed him. "Dad, take me with you!"

The words tumbled out of my small mouth. He ignored me, kept carrying the black bags to his car. At the door, I tried to follow, but he stopped and turned. "You go with your mom," he said.

I didn't understand. Then the tears came. I stood at the screen door and cried as he drove away. I cried until my face burned and tears and snot mixed into a salty mess.

Angie tells me that we ended up moving in with Ita so Mom could rent the house for extra money. The timeline is fuzzy. The stories here haven't been told to me enough to create a memory. I just remember being with Angie and Ita a lot because Mom was working two part-time jobs trying to make ends meet.

"You know, Mom worked the graveyard shift as an operator at Southwestern General part-time. She'd get off at six a.m., come home and shower, then go and work the front desk at the Orthopedic Center until noon. That just shows how much Mom wanted to make it. You know?" Angie turns to look at me.

I nod. My chest aches as I see my mom's petite frame wrapped in exhaustion all the time. I know that face from when she worked double shifts or graveyard with Customs. How grateful she was to have a job even if it was tainted with irony. Mom, the brown gatekeeper to other brown people.

It also explains why it's always Angie and Ita in my memories before first grade, then just a lot of Ita as Angie got older. It shows me why Mom always said, "The only person I can rely on is me." Even though Ita was there to help, Mom saw her as someone else she had to take care of.

Even when she wasn't there, Mom took care of us all.

EIGHT

MY DAD HAD just dropped me off at Ita's. It was after I'd spent a day at his house. My dad's house was a small building behind his parents' house. He'd moved there after Mom had kicked him out. My mom told me she wouldn't let me be second to my half-sister and two half-brothers. I don't think this helped, though.

It was one of the few times I'd been with him after the divorce. I was eight years old. He'd already left me waiting a handful of times, so when he'd actually showed up this time at Ita's house, I was surprised and relieved.

The drive home that Sunday was quiet with only the radio playing. I stared out the window as we drove from the Northeast toward Central. I liked Central better.

He asked if I'd had fun. I nodded.

I eyeballed his stocky body behind the steering wheel and a memory of when I'd been younger flashed through my mind. I'd been small enough that he'd let me sit in his lap and let me believe I'd steered us out of the driveway, his round beer belly squeezed against my back, the smell of Old Spice in my nose as I giggled.

I wanted to hang on to that memory, but when we got to my grandma's, he sat, double parked, waiting for me to get out. I was just about to run up the twenty-five concrete stairs of Ita's house when I tripped. I crashed into the grainy cement, my head connecting with the edge of the first step, right at the center of my forehead.

It took a minute for the pain to sink in. I lay face down against the ground, staring at the concrete's mica glinting bright at me. I'd been running back to my grandma, to comfort, and now I lay on the ground, dirty, fragments of skull floating away from my brain, the air knocked out of me. It felt as if my head might break apart like an eggshell, but I couldn't cry. The tears were stuck deep in the pit of my stomach, a feeling I'd grown accustomed to since my parents divorced, and my father had left.

I didn't hear him get out of the car, but there he was suddenly, picking me up off the ground just as I finally let out a wail. Through the pain, I heard the screen door at the top of the stairs slam and bounce against its frame.

"¿Qué le hiciste?" Ita yelled moving down the stairs from the porch.

What did he do to me? My dad looked up from his large brown hands which were wrapped around my forehead. The years he'd spent as a carpenter left his hands filled with mounds of calluses, thick, translucent layers of skin. It felt like his fleshy hands were the only thing keeping the eggshell pieces of my head together.

"Estaba corriendo y se tropezó. ¡Se pegó en la frente!"

He tried to explain that I'd just tripped, but in explaining he loosened his grip on my head and I cried out. The pain didn't stop, sharp and hard in my head, trying to make its way out, pushing and shoving. My dad's hands held on, his fingers gripping my forehead, holding my brains in, keeping me from falling apart. My tears came in waves, rushed out of my chest and mouth, finally finding an escape from the pressure.

"¿Cómo que se tropezó?" Ita asked, left eyebrow raised.

What do you mean she tripped? Their words swam around me. My grandma reached out and her arms encircled me, pulled me away from my dad, from his calloused hands, and hugged me hard, my face pressed into her cotton tank top, into the soft, salty flesh of her stomach and breasts.

"She was running, and she fell, I don't know how she tripped," he rushed out in one breath.

I couldn't see, still squished against my grandma. I had to imagine his thick hands, palms open in the air, trying to explain to her.

"A ver, Prieta, déjame ver," she said, prying me away.

Cool air hit my face, and a new wave of pain struck me. I started to cry again, snot running out of my nose and mingling in with my spit, when I heard her talking about the hospital. I didn't want to go to the hospital. I hiccupped short gasps of salty air as they talked. My grandma was going to call my mom. When my dad offered to take us to the emergency room, I inhaled a big breath of air. Ita let me out of her embrace and started up the stairs.

I peered, standing alone for a moment as she took the stairs in quick short bursts, trying to muffle my cries. My dad put his arm, heavy, around my shoulders as we walked toward his Monte Carlo. He put me in the center of the front seat to wait for Ita. The dashboard shone from layers of Armor All.

I shut my eyes for a second, but he shook me and said, "Don't go to sleep, mija!" I held them open, watched his face to focus. His black beard and frowning eyebrows pointed up in the center, like mine. I wondered about him, this man who was my father.

How uncomfortable I felt around him now. The family we had been drifted further and further away.

My parents' divorce wouldn't be final for another year, but even before then the memory of them living together was like a picture left in the sun: it kept fading. My dad still tried to see me during a small window of time after my mom served him with the papers. That window quickly shut, though. I didn't really understand why things changed.

I'm not sure I do even now.

They'd lived apart since I was three, except on weekends. Then we were all together—Angie, half-sister Geno, two half-brothers Manny and Louie, Mom and Dad and me—like a family, all of us squished in his '85 Monte Carlo, elbows and knees jabbing into one another. We sang along with Bobby Darin and with Little Anthony and the Imperials on 92.3 the Fox as my dad drove us to the Sunday swap near Fox Plaza, a place on the south side of the highway where more people spoke Spanish than English. There I drank limonada, fresh squeezed and served out of a big glass jar with a metal ladle into an oversize Styrofoam cup. I ate corn layered in a cup with butter, lime, white crumbled cheese, chili powder and Valentina hot sauce. At the end of the day, though, after the limonadas and corn, my mom, Angie, and I went to our house, and they went to theirs.

I never saw my parents fight. I was surprised when Mom spelled out *divorce* in front of me, like I didn't know how to spell. Even before that, I knew our family was different just from listening to the things other kids said at school. Some just had just a mom, some just a dad, some both, but they had them all the time, half the time, or none of the time, nothing like mine. We were a weekend family. I didn't know anyone else like me. I guess all those years of weekend family time gave my dad hope they would get back together.

Then, after the divorce, my father slowly disappeared until, *poof*.

I have a hard time piecing together the disjointed memories I have of him.

But this one—the day I fell on the concrete stairs—is the clearest.

I turned away from him and looked up at the stairs, glad to see my grandma race down to rescue me. I'd stopped crying, but I still leaned into her and felt the warmth of her body against mine.

"Vamos al Southwester, está cerquita," my grandma said, smoothing my hair back.

Neither of them talked. I sniffled loudly, each sniff louder and louder, echoing off the fabric seats, bouncing off the shiny Armor All dashboard, only to land on a wrinkle of my dad's brow, then my grandma's, the frowns on their faces filled with reverberated sniffs. My dad reached for the knob on the radio, then jerked back and placed his hand back on the steering wheel. We were a block away from Southwestern General Hospital. I was glad the ride was short even if I didn't want to go.

She studied my forehead and what I imagined to be a golf ball sized bump. "Qué buen chingazo te diste, Prieta. Gracias a Dios que no te abriste la frente. ¿Pero cómo pasó?"

Whenever I hurt myself, my grandma always thanked God that what happened was not worse than it could have been. This time I had to agree it was great I didn't bust open my forehead either.

"I don't know, Ita. I was running, I blinked and just tripped," I said.

She gave my dad a sideways glance. He didn't turn his head. He kept his eyes fixed on the road.

"My dad was waiting in the car for me to get upstairs," I finished.

I didn't say anything else. Neither did she. Her eyes just kept darting from my forehead to the street. I didn't want to touch my face. The skin on my forehead felt tight and throbbed.

When the car stopped to let us out, Ita asked, "¿No se va parquear?" She turned, eyes wide. *He wasn't going to park?*

The car idled for a few moments before he answered. "Sí, sí claro."

He turned the steering wheel and backed up into a parking spot, front end facing forward. His face and brows were furrowed into deep ridges. He backed inch by inch into a spot with no other cars around it.

They both got out of the car. I didn't move.

"Vente, Prieta."

I slid out of the car, my hand dragging along the upholstery, my fingers making light blue lines against the grain of the fabric until I had to let go. My grandma ducked down by the edge of the car door. "Ya vente, Prieta." I grabbed her hand.

"Are you her mother?" a dark-haired nurse asked Ita.

"No, her grandmother."

"Okay." She paused, looking between the two of us. "We need a guardian with her at all times though. Is her mother or father here?"

Ita and I both turned to look at my dad, but his gaze just moved between the three of us: Ita, me, and the nurse. Silent.

"Her mother is on her way," Ita rushed. "She was at work. Her father is here, but—"

"I want my Ita . . ."

"Her father is leaving." My grandma looked at me and nodded where only I could see—in her eyes. "Her mother should be here any minute."

The nurse glanced between my red, splotchy face and my grandma's. We didn't look at each other or at her, and we didn't say anything.

"Can her father sign off before he leaves? We can get her examined while we're waiting for her mother to arrive. Meanwhile, you can stay with your granddaughter, Mrs.—"

"Acosta," Ita replied.

"Does that sound good, sweetheart?" She smiled at me, all teeth showing. I didn't like it. Her smile, which seemed too big, tightened the corners of her mouth as she filled out the paperwork on her clipboard.

That day my dad had tried to make pork chops for me, the way I liked them, fried crispy with salt and pepper flakes almost burnt onto the deep brown meat. My mom had told him they were my favorite. I hadn't said anything when he served them burnt. I only watched thc fuzzy TV in the corner of the cramped living room as he drank the Coors Light he nestled between his legs when he wasn't drinking from it.

"¿Están buenas, mija?"

I nodded, nibbling on the blackened edges, and stared up at my smiling face in the kindergarten photo hung on his wall. I looked happy.

After lunch, I played with my cousins. My dad had called his brother to tell him to drop them off. We played hide and seek and hung from the mulberry tree in his parents' front yard, trying to get close to the cicadas, or chicharras, as we called them, as they sang to us. My cousins giggled at jokes I didn't understand and asked where I'd been. I shrugged and tried to climb farther up the tree. Dad watched with my grandfather, Papi Polo, and drank beer, each taking turns at the fridge as Mami Paola, my grandmother, cooked flautas, my cousins' favorite.

When the nurse walked out, the sound of the curtain made me turn and look at my grandma. She wasn't going anywhere, was she?

"No te preocupes, Prieta. No, me voy a ir a ningún lado. Y 'orita va llegar tu mama." She nodded, her head reinforcing her words.

She squeezed my hand with her warm one and sat back down in the chair next to the white bed I lay on. She talked to me about her day. I held her hand and poked at the extended ball of vein on its back. She knew I wasn't listening, but I didn't want her to stop, her voice a warm blanket in this cold, sterile curtained room.

Nothing like Mami Paola's voice.

Papi Polo was much nicer. While my cousins and I played in the yard that day, an ice cream truck drove by. I heard the little song from blocks away.

"Can we please have ice cream, Dad?" He laughed, nodded his head, and dug in his pocket.

We each got an ice cream, mine a bomb pop. My cousins also bought small red earrings with their own money, trinkets made from small metal upholstery nails, the tops painted different colors with nail polish, the points of the shaft dulled with no backing and still a little sharp, but I wanted them. I didn't have an allowance yet and ran back with only my ice cream. I stared at their earrings, the music moving away house by house, when Papi Polo held out a dollar, "Tenga, mija," and gestured with his chin toward the truck. He held his hand out to hold my ice cream. I got my own earrings, pink little metal circles, and he let me keep the change. My dad came out with two more beers, a flauta in his mouth, and Mami Paola who *tsked* at the ice cream.

"Look, Dad!" I held out the pink earrings.

"¡Qué bonitos, mija! Se te van a ver muy bonitos."

Later, in the bathroom, I took my small gold hoops out, and put them in my pocket. Careful not to poke myself, I put the small, pink-painted metal nails in my ears and turned my head from left to right, looking in the mirror.

At the hospital, I played with the pink earrings, careful not to touch the sharp back. The doctor came in and asked what had happened, then made me follow a flashlight with my eyes.

"That's quite a bump you got there," he said, face inches from mine. His breath smelled of minty gum.

I peered to the side of his head to avoid his eyes.

"Mrs. Acosta—you're her grandmother, yes?"

"Yes, sir."

"We're going to take her to run some tests, make sure she doesn't have a concussion. You can come with her and as soon as her mother gets here, we can update her on everything. But, for right now, she doesn't seem to have anything too serious. We just want to confirm."

"Okay, thank you very much, doctor," she said, shaking her head, still holding my hand. "You know how kids are. She scared me to death, you know."

My dad had signed the papers before he left and told my grandma he'd call to check on me. They took me to different rooms in a wheelchair, my grandma alongside me the whole way. People stared at me, and my cheeks burned. The chichón felt like it was huge and hot as another doctor examined it and gently touched the area.

"Ita, when's Mom getting here?"

"'Orita llega, Prieta. Ya sabes cómo se mantiene de ocupado el puente."

Paso del Norte Bridge, where my mom was that day,

was the busier port of entry. Although my mom worked at all the bridges depending on how shifts or overtime were rotated, she always came home a little more tired from that bridge. When we got back from my tests, my mom was there, barking out questions at Ita.

"¡Mamá! ¿Qué pasó? ¿Cómo se cayó? ¿Dónde está Chuy?"

She was in full uniform, her gun still hung on her hip. She pulled me into her arms, my face squished into the buttons of her scratchy navy shirt, badge cool against my skin. She squeezed me hard, but I didn't say anything when she asked for my dad. My mom's voice was wound up like a tightly twisted wire. Ita explained what happened.

"Gorda, está bien. Estamos esperando unos exámenes, pero dijo el doctor que no piensa que tenga una contusión."

"Mom, I'm okay," I mumbled against her chest.

She loosened her grip on me. "You sure? Mija, look at your forehead! Does it hurt still?"

She squinted into my face.

"What are these?" She pulled at the pink earrings. "Ay!" She jerked her hand away and rubbed her thumb against the tips of her fingers.

"Papi Polo bought them for me from the ice cream man."

"You can wear them later," she said, smiling a little, taking them out, careful with her fingers. "You don't need to stab yourself today too." She set them next to me on the rolling tray table then pulled me against her again. "Ay, mija, you have to be more careful!"

I nodded into her body.

"¿Y su papá?"

The pink earrings rocked back and forth against the

table. I squished my face against her harder as she asked for my dad again.

"Pues, se fue."

There was a long silence in the room, and we heard only the beeps and footsteps outside our curtain. Her arms stiffened as I squeezed my eyes shut against the last bit of light.

NINE

I ALMOST CUT my left thumb off when I was in the third grade. My teacher, Mrs. Vickers, assigned the class to bring a clean three-liter jug of soda so we could make an ecosystem. At home, I was glad we had an almost empty three-liter waiting for me. The clean part proved more difficult. I should have asked for help. I should have waited for my mom to do it for me. I should have done that, but I didn't. Instead, I tried to take the Coke label off myself. With a chef's knife.

We were in the kitchen, but because our counters made a big beige C shape, my mom's back was to me as she went through the mail. She has always had a problem with mail. She lets it pile up. She pays bills, then just lets the paper sit there until it stacks into large crooked piles that she won't throw away until she goes through them. Again. When we cleaned out her storage unit in 2016, Angie and I found boxes of it.

I. Hate. Mail.

As Mom read through it, I stood in the kitchen holding the three-liter with my left hand and the knife with my right. It was surely the best way to take off the label. I slid the pointed tip of the blade underneath the top of the label and pushed down. The waxy paper ripped just a bit, but not all the way.

So I did it again.

I raised the large chef's knife and sliced down. *Ohhh!* It took me a moment to realize what I'd done, even though I felt a pain in my hand. When I looked, I saw blood beginning to seep out of the sliced meaty skin between my index finger and thumb. I had slashed a straight line right through the webbing between the two.

I turned quick to see if Mom had seen.

"Don't use the knife to cut the label off, Yasmín," is what she'd told me minutes before.

But I hadn't been able to find scissors so, when I saw she was glued to the stack of white envelopes in front of her, I did exactly what she said I shouldn't do.

I slapped my right hand over the cut and ran to the bathroom. She'd be so mad if she saw it! Hot tears spilled from my eyes as I ran water over my hand. I rinsed and rinsed the pink cyclone of water down the drain, but my hand wouldn't stop bleeding.

Panic seeped up into my chest. My mom was going to find out what I did. I rinsed and rinsed but more blood blossomed from the wound. Blood was all over the white sink and seemed to be spreading. *How was I going to hide this?*

Mymomisgonnabemad. Mymomisgonnabemad. Mymomisgonnabemad.

That's when I heard the knock. "Mija, what are you doing?"

I didn't answer. I didn't know what to say. Lucky for me,

my mom didn't allow locked doors at home. The silence told her plenty. She slammed into the bathroom.

"What did you do!" she yelled.

I hiccupped a big gulp of air.

"Yasmín!"

"I-I c-cut mmm-yself!"

She turned off the water and pulled the towel off the rack.

"I told you not to use the knife! Didn't I! Te dije!"

She pulled at my arm and pressed the towel against my wet, bloody hand. She pushed the thick cloth hard against the bleeding flesh.

"Why didn't you tell me?!"

"I-I didn't want y-you to get m-mad."

Her face changed. The straight line of her mouth fell open, making an O. The deep furrow between her brows flattened. The hard look in her eyes vanished as quickly as the blood that rushed down the drain.

"Mija," she said, pulling me into her arms.

I cried into the stiff shirt of her uniform. Even though her badge dug into my cheek, I didn't pull away. I hugged her with my right arm. She still held the towel against my left hand as she held me and let me cry. When my chest stopped heaving, she pulled away from me.

"Let me see how deep it is."

I nodded and winced as she unwrapped the blood-soaked towel.

"Ay, mija!"

Her voice was so loud, I jumped. She took a deep breath and exhaled.

"You did a job on it."

The bleeding had stopped so she could see just how deep I had cut myself. I sat on the bathroom toilet as she cleaned and bandaged the skin.

When I look at my hand now, I can't find the scar. It must have faded, or all the other lines on my palm swallowed it up. Scars arc funny things because even after they've disappeared, they still leave an invisible mark.

TEN

THERE WAS ONLY one bathroom at Ita's house. It was pink. Ita's bathrooms were always pink. Pepto Bismol pink. It's ironic that Ita chose this color for the bathroom since she had so much trouble with her stomach. Ulcerative colitis. A fun disease she inherited from her mother that caused long-lasting inflammation and ulcers on her digestive tract. She spent *a lot* of time in the bathroom. Once it was diagnosed, Ita very slowly gave up many things that caused her stomach irritation, like alcohol and greasy foods, but she had the hardest time giving up chile. Salsas with their jalapeño or chile de arbol spice—she just couldn't go without it even though it caused her so much pain.

The bathroom had a big old porcelain clawfoot bathtub. It wasn't until I was older and we had a shower at Mom's house that I realized the act of taking a bath, not just bathing to be clean, was a bit of a ritual in our family and took an endless amount of time. Even a "quick" bath—when Ita filled the tub for me just a little, and I soaped myself up, then tried my best to rinse—took more time than a shower.

Ita even added an *I Can't Believe It's Not Butter!* container (aka Mexican Tupperware) that sat propped between the tub and the pink wall so we could scoop the water up and over ourselves to rinse off better. In the summer, these types of baths provided a bit of relief from the oppressive heat. In the winter, they were miserable and filled with goose-bumped chicken skin even with the old red-coiled space heater buzzing in the corner of the narrow bathroom.

Often, with just the two of us, I swam around in the tub while Ita got ready or used the toilet. I loved taking baths. The small audience of Ita never bothered me. I had a little plastic blue shower cap I put on my head to keep my hair dry—washing my *long* hair was another feat in itself. I'd float in that tub for an hour or longer if she'd let me. I'd lay on my belly and kick my little legs as if I was in a swimming pool until my fingers and toes turned into little tan prunes. I loved that bathtub. Now I miss it.

The inverse happened when Ita took a bath. Sometimes I just wanted to sit with her while she bathed. She never minded. Ita's baths were different though because she added Skin So Soft bath oil. The air was moist with humidity and Avon's herbal scent for Ita's baths. It made me think our bathroom was now in the Doris Day movie *Pillow Talk* that Ita and I had seen. Fancy and luxurious.

When I was little, I never noticed Ita's naked body. It was just Ita. As I grew older, I saw more. Ita's skin, always well moisturized, was littered with scars. Long horizontal and vertical incisions bleached white against already pale skin.

When I was older, I sometimes lingered in the bathroom after I used the toilet if Ita happened to be standing up in the tub, ready to get out. Drops of water clung to her skin. She didn't seem to care that I was sharing the same space with her as she dried her arms, rubbed at her armpits, stomach, and crotch, raised her breast to dry underneath. She'd rest her foot on the curled white edge of the tub to dry one leg, then the other. She'd pull the mint green towel across her back and tug left, right, left, right again. She'd clutch the towel to her chest, gripping the tub's smooth curled edge and stepping out of the tub, her skin still glistening from the bath oil. It was just a moment really, then she'd look up at me as if asking, "You still here?" I'd quickly fold the squares of toilet paper and wipe, but not before she turned to wrap the towel around her and I could see the long waxy scar along her lower spine.

Why did Ita have so many scars?

These intimate moments with my Ita stuck with me. After lots of questions, I was able to piece together my own stories with Mom's and Angie's to figure out where all those scars came from.

The Back

Ita was twenty-nine when she worked at TexTox, a textile factory located off Texas Avenue in Central El Paso. She worked her way up from sewing machine operator to line supervisor in a short amount of time. She was very proud of getting the position because she had been promoted over people with high school diplomas. Ita had only gone to school through the eighth grade at Bowie High. She'd tried several times to go back for her GED, but something about the classroom made her fidget in her seat. In fact, she fidgeted so much she fidgeted right out of the small wooden desks, down the hallway, and through the front door.

While she was working at TexTox, she tried to move a large bundle of denim fabric out of the way by bending down to pick it up as she had always done in the past, only this time she couldn't get up. Panicked, she called out for help. At the hospital, doctors told her she had slipped a disk in her back. She needed surgery. After this, TexTox strung Ita along. They told her she still had a "job," but didn't pay her. It was 1960 and Ita got lost with their reasons because none of them put food on the table for her children. Mom and Tío were just eight and seven at the time, so when I asked what happened, they both shrugged.

So then Ita worked at another factory, but that soon closed.

Ita always went where there was work. She called bingo in the colonia of Anapra, a poor outlying rural part of Juárez. She created her own concession stand with my thirteen-year-old mom who helped her sell chili beans and hot dogs at cockfights in the same neighborhood. She was a waitress, a laundromat assistant, and even did retail at Korean stores in downtown El Paso. She often worked two jobs at a time to support my mom and Tío. She had to make enough to support her family *and* pay for childcare because Mamá Lupe refused to help. She never approved of Ita's marriage. She judged her even more harshly after Ita was divorced.

Ita could never win with Mamá Lupe.

Ita was often alone. The fairy-tale man she yearned for never appeared. My mom remembers Ita working lots of different jobs up until Mom was fifteen. At that time, Ita got her first job as a bartender at a place called El Azteca. That's when Ita discovered she could make more money bartending.

Down the middle of her lower back, she had a five-inch scar. As she got older, her back issues worsened. She suffered from pain in her neck and back from degenerative disc disorder, wear and tear from all the jobs she'd had. The weight of all her memories grew too heavy for her to carry. Her last years were plagued with chronic distress. Endless white-topped orange medicine bottles cluttered her dresser but didn't do much to relieve her pain.

The Ankle

She had small white scars on her ankle. These were left from large metal needles that were inserted after she hemorrhaged from an ectopic pregnancy when she was thirty years old.

That was her last pregnancy.

They lived on 815 N. El Paso when it happened. Mom and Tío sat with Ita's husband Tony in the hospital waiting room. Mom was only eight years old but remembers wondering what would happen to them if Ita died. Ita had always kept them safe. The doctor had just told them, "We've done all we can. She's a fighter, but the next seventy-two hours are critical. The rest is in God's hands."

Little did the doctor know how familiar Ita was with God's hands.

The Hysterectomy

After seven miscarriages and the ectopic pregnancy, Ita had a total hysterectomy at thirty-seven. The scar along her abdomen was faded. I hardly remember it. She never spoke about it. My mom told me she'd had to have it done because she was having endless periods. I imagine her changing bloodied pads day after day, rolling the length of the red-stained cotton and wondering what was happening to her body, each bloodied pad her penance.

I don't know when Ita became religious or if she always was. Every Sunday, we went to church. We prayed nightly. She prayed mostly. Hard. Her eyelids clinging to one another, her brow furrowed. Her lips moved too fast to make out the words. Her hands clasped together in her lap. She prayed, and I never knew why.

Saying "Life was hard for my grandma" in English doesn't suffice. The words lack feeling. In this case, Español tiene más sentimiento. *Le tocó muy dura la vida a mi Ita.* She believed the hardships of her life were her penance. I think Ita prayed for seven deep scars no one ever saw. She prayed for mistakes and self-doubt, the weight heavy. Mostly she prayed that she had made the right choices all those years ago.

The Forehead

Ita was thirty-nine when an argument turned physical. She ended up with a scar on her forehead where a widow's peak would have been. The fight, I imagine from the stories I've been told, takes place in a green-walled living room. Ita always painted her living rooms a shade of pistachio green.

The fight starts when she yells, wondering where he's been, how much he's been drinking. He, Gil, tries to walk away from her, but she swings.

He ducks. His breath, tinged with beer and cigarettes, fills the room.

"Mamita, ya, todo está bien," he says.

He calls her mamita and wraps his arms around her, pinning her arms to her sides. He holds her like he will never let her go, and, in a way, he never did. The words and the actions don't match. They show the twisted way Gil loved my Ita. It also shows how, even though she wanted love more than anything, Ita didn't know how to be loved because even after this, she still stayed with him.

Gil drank his way in and out of her life until the day she died. Even after she was gone, neighbors called my mom to tell her a homeless-looking man had been peeking in the windows of my Ita's house. From the description, she knew it was Gil. "How could he outlive my mom?" she asked me. "No es justo."

I stay quiet when she says this. Although part of me agrees with my mom, I wanted to ask if someone's death was ever justified. I know Ita's still doesn't make sense to me now.

Even after all of this.

Gil keeps his arms around her in a tight bear hug. Ita struggles, trying to pry herself out of his grip, away from the bitter smell of alcohol. "Déjame, cabrón," she yells, but he keeps his arms where they are. He knows if he lets go, her left hand will come out swinging. Instead he throws his head forward, headbutting her.

Smack.

The sound of two stubborn heads echoes through the house and silences the argument for a moment. Ita is dazed and wonders if it's possible to get drunk just from smelling his breath. Gil's head stings, but he doesn't let go. A small bead of blood runs down the center of Ita's forehead. "Ya mamita, ya," he says, his voice low, loving, as if he was comforting her.

The Gallbladder

The removal of her gallbladder at age thirty-nine marked the beginning of many of Ita's stomach issues. It left a mean jagged scar across the right side of her stomach. It made me wonder how big a gallbladder was and why it had been so dysfunctional that it demanded to be gone. Stomach issues run in the family. Mamá Lupe, Ita, my sister. Angie, who looks the most like my Ita, has problems with her stomach and has already had her gallbladder removed too. Her stomach gets angry frequently. She jokes when she has attacks triggered by things like MSG, oats, high fat, fried foods, wheat. I have my chile-loving fingers crossed that I, at least, inherited my gallbladder from my dad's side of the family and not my mom's.

Seriously, chile es vida.

Later, my Ita had portions of her intestine removed because of frequent issues with colitis. She was banned from eating anything spicy. This was a source of sadness not just for her but for me. Ita had trained me in the ways of making spicy chile. Now we would no longer share our spicy bond.

As a child, I watched as she'd toast the chile, onion, and tomatoes, then peel the black blistered skin from them. I helped at this point, careful not to touch my eyes. Sometimes my small fingers burned like when my hand fell asleep, and it felt like ants were waking it up.

She squished the three with a small glass she saved from Doña María mole to make salsa. I watched, ready with a tostada to taste-test the finished product. When she was done, she'd wash away the small red and black pieces that clung to her hands, rubbing olive oil on them to kill the sting.

I thought about this memory when I called her after I'd moved away and asked how to get the skin off the chile and tomato more easily. I thought about how she must have missed the spicy flavor.

Now I think of how much I miss cooking with her.

The Mastectomy

At forty-two, Ita had a burning sensation on her breast. She touched the skin quick, swatting as if a bug had bitten her, but instead her fingers found a small lump. After talking with my mom, visiting the doctor, and having a biopsy, the diagnosis was confirmed: cancer. Her right breast was removed soon after. She was left with a bright pink diagonal scar against soft white skin. For a long time, she was depressed. She wasn't quick to joke or make up her own words to songs like usual.

Instead, she grieved the loss of her womanhood and beauty at the same time. I imagine her sitting in her pistachio living room staring blankly at the novelas she wasn't really watching.

As a child, I watched her adjust the silky skin of the soft prosthesis in the pocket sewn in her bra. I saw the bleached scar on her skin. To me, it was normal that Ita didn't have a breast. I didn't question it but remember the look on her face as she smoothed her tops, eyes focused on her chest, her waist, as she turned, smoothed, turned, and smoothed again before we ever left the house.

The Nose

At fifty-two, Ita had her nose broken as she tried to break up a fight between her friend Suzi and her man—her viejo—Mike. They had been out partying in Juárez and hit the part of the night when arguments erupt and fists fly freely.

Mike and Suzi began to argue. Mike started to give chingazos a la Suzi. Who knows why he was hitting her, but Ita jumped in to help. Mike punched her square in the face. Knuckles exploded against her nose.

Crunch!

The drinks and adrenaline dulled the sound of crushed cartilage as Ita swung back with her own chingazos. A lefty, she always caught her opponents off guard. The result was a bruised and beaten Mike, Suzi, and Ita.

Her nose was never set. Sinusitis plagued her for the rest of her life, but at least she didn't have a flattened boxer nose.

There was that, right?

When I ask my mom about this, she gives me a few small details and says she doesn't remember much. She sounds dismissive. Her voice asks me, without asking, why I want to know about this. I don't answer.

The Ruptured Vein

As a child, this was my favorite scar. I thought it was magic. At one of her visits to the hospital, a nurse ruptured the vein on the top of her hand while she was attempting to give Ita an IV. No one remembers why Ita was at the hospital or how old she was. I asked my mom and sister, but both just remember it happened suddenly like that. Sometimes I hear my Ita's voice beginning to tell me the story of the vein, but her voice fades as quickly as my mind tries to grasp the memory.

After the visit to the hospital, the center of her right hand had a green-tinged bubble. When I pushed it down with my small index finger, it magically sprung back as soon as I lifted it. When she held her hand up in the air, it flattened down and seemed regular, like mine. I poked at it endlessly until she said, "Ya, Prieta, ya," and pulled her hand away from me. My little fingers still itched to touch it again, so I'd wait until she got distracted watching *Wheel of Fortune* to start poking once more.

ELEVEN

Manuel R. Lopez

"I think he and your Ita got married in '51. My mom was twenty, and he was twenty-two. They got married here in El Paso, but then left for Los Angeles for him to find a job. I think they stayed with my aunt Sally till they got their own place. I'm not sure though."

I typed as Mom and I spoke over the phone. I interviewed her to learn more about her childhood and about my grandma's love life and marriages. Family stories get mixed up and timelines jumbled. I needed to know more about Ita.

"And then?" I asked. "What else do you remember about your dad?"

"Well, they were together for a couple years. She had your uncle and me. I was only fifteen days old when he came home after being out all night. He and your Ita were arguing as they walked up the stairs to our apartment—you know how your grandma was—and he turned and punched her. My mom almost fell down the stairs except a neighbor came out to check on the noise, and your Ita fell against him. If not? He would have killed my mom."

"So he punched Ita? And she almost fell down the stairs?" My fingers hung over the keys as I waited for her answer.

"Yes, that's why your Ita kicked him out." I imagined my mother nodding on the other end. "My mom had it after that. It wasn't the first time this happened, you know? She went upstairs and got one of your uncle's metal roller toys, the kind with two wheels. When it was rolled, little balls inside a dome bounced around."

I could tell she was gesturing with her hands.

"And she went to town on him. Then she went to town on his car, broke out the headlights, cracked the windshield. He left for El Paso that night, and they said—I don't know if this is true—that he showed up with a black eye and a broken arm."

Salvador Moreno

"I think your Ita met him when I was a year, maybe a year-and-half. We were still in L.A. Salvador treated Mom like an angel. Mamá Lupe said he was a good man, affectionate with your uncle and me. It meant a lot to your Ita that Mamá Lupe finally approved of someone.

"Or—of anything.

"I don't remember him well because we were pretty young, but Ita said he carried me everywhere we went. I don't know how long they courted, but when they got married, he got jealous and possessive. When they were married, they ran into the donor and his vieja—"

"The donor? You mean, your dad?" I asked.

"Yes, the donor."

There was silence on the other end.

"And then?" I finally asked.

"They were at a market in L.A. and got into it. Salvador beat the crap out of the donor. '¿Cómo le saben los chingazos de un hombre?' Salvador asked after the donor was all bloodied up."

There was something poetic about Salvador asking how being beat up by a man felt since it seemed Manuel hadn't hesitated to hit Ita. Even though Salvador ended up being a horrible man because of how he became obsessed with my grandma, I savored this part of the story of him beating up "the donor," and hoped it was true.

"So, Salvador beat up your dad in the middle of a market in L.A., and nothing happened? How did your dad end up back in L.A.?" I asked.

"I don't know how he ended back there, mija . . ."—she paused—" . . . oh, they arrested Salvador and your Ita, but then they let them go because the donor didn't press charges. She and Salvador were happy—aside from that incident. It wasn't until later when she found out what Salvador was really like, and she left for El Paso."

"What do you mean?" I asked.

"I don't really know. He killed Robert Perales here in El Paso, so maybe they came back together," Mom said, talking more to herself than me.

"Salvador killed someone while he was married to Ita?"

"I don't know when they came back to El Paso. But, yes, he was in jail for killing Perales when your Ita filed for divorce, and that's when he broke out of jail. They say he jumped out of the window and broke both ankles, but back then prisoners wore combat boots so he strapped them tighter and went after your grandma. I don't know how he found out where we lived or how he got a gun. I remember my mom trying to keep us close, and we moved around a lot but still . . ."

"So, he found you guys? And . . . ?" I typed, the phone pinched between my right ear and shoulder.

"He came to the door, and your Ita shoved me away. She tried to push the door closed on him. He pointed the gun at your Ita and fired, but the gun was so well oiled, it kept slipping. She grabbed your uncle and me and ran. After the shootout with the cops, they found him lying face up, bent from the knees with a hole in the back of his head, the same way he'd killed Robert Perales. I remember the blood on my little white shoe. It'd fallen on the ground when your grandma ran toward the police. Thank God, que no mató a mi mamá."

My keys stayed quiet for a moment.

Pete Guevara

"She was already with Pete when Salvador tried to kill her. They met at TexTox, the manufacturing company she worked at in Central. Around Cotton and Texas Avenue. They made all kinds of clothes. I don't remember a lot about Pete."

"Was he nicer than the others?" I hoped for a good answer.

"Well, they fought. One time they got into an argument, and he grabbed a dinner knife, and my mom grabbed a fork and stabbed him on the side of the head. When he tried to punch it out with your grandma, he always got the raw end of the deal. Always got laid out. He couldn't outbox her. And my mom? Nada. And Pete wasn't a small man. He just wasn't fast enough for her. Aside from the fights, they liked to go out dancing, drinking. They liked to party. The funny part is their fights only happened when they were sober."

"When I was about six, we lived on North El Paso Street, 811, that was it, and they were separated. She caught him with another woman and filed for divorce."

"That's it?"

"Yeah, mija. That's all I remember."

Tony Bustamante

"I was seven or eight when they first got together. Tony was a hunk." Mom laughed big from her belly. Her deep cackle came through loud on the phone. "He was a paratrooper in the army, instructor, I think, a master sergeant. Here at Ft. Bliss."

"How did they meet?"

"I think my mom knew his brother Henry, and they met through him. We moved to 815 North El Paso Street a little farther up, and Pete came looking for my mom when she and Tony were married, but it was too late.

"They were very happy. My mom was very happy. We went to picnics. She was with him for a while. By then, I was eleven. Hmm, I hadn't realized they'd been together that long." Mom paused for a moment, and I stayed quiet. I didn't want to interrupt her memories.

"It's the happiest I remember seeing my mom. She said he was the love of her life."

"What happened?" I asked.

"When she was pregnant with that ectopic pregnancy, she almost died. She had a hemorrhage, and her tube ruptured. But my mom was a little fighter. When she came home, things were normal for a while, but then things changed. I think maybe it was all too much."

José Luis Santoyo

"They lived together for a couple of years. I was about thirteen. He lost his job and left town to find work, and we were supposed to move with him wherever he found work, but she never heard from him again. My mom really liked him. He was really sweet to her, too nice maybe." Mom's voice was wistful and far away.

"When he got back, she was already with Choco. José said he'd written her letters, proposing, but she never got them. They stayed friends till she passed away."

Pablo "Choco" Garcia

"I don't remember how old I was when they got together," she said. "He worked for Asarco—the smelting plant? I think they met when my mom was working as a bartender at the D'Carlo downtown. I don't really remember anything about him. They didn't fight like the others. When they were living together, she found out he was married, and they split up because he wouldn't get a divorce."

"But why?"

"Who knows?" I imagined her shrugging on the other end of the phone. "They got back together after your Ita left Gil for a little bit—a year, maybe a year and a half, but that was it."

Gilberto Contreras

"She met Gil at the Azteca, bartending there too. They started going out. Gil wasn't bad-looking, and he really spoiled her.

When they first started dating, Tony found my mom at the Azteca and set a date to meet with her. But somebody gave Gil the heads-up. He showed up there, and your Ita couldn't leave to meet Tony. Gil was always jealous, but not as much as the others."

"Why didn't she just leave?" I asked.

"I don't know, mija. I guess it just wasn't meant to be."

"What else about Gil? What do you remember?" I had only known Gil later in life, when his face had grown bumpy with craters from the alcohol. But I wondered what he had been like before then, when his face was bright, and they both smiled at the camera in black and white photos, looking like the perfect '50s greaser couple.

"When they were married, they were happy, as long as they weren't drinking. When he drank, he turned into a real asshole. They got into a big fight when I was pregnant with your sister, and I hit Gil with the handset of the telephone, and my mom told me not to get involved. He wasn't stupid though. He didn't try to duke it out with your grandma. He'd hit her, then hug her so she couldn't hit him. That's how he headbutted her and left that scar on her forehead. They got divorced, I can't remember when, but Gil never really left her alone. Well, you remember, don't you, mija?"

I nodded at the other end of the phone. Remembering the story—the neighbor telling us about a homeless man peeking through the windows of her house a year after she had died. Ita had always been an anchor for Gil. Now I imagined he floated around even more aimlessly than usual, a can of Natural Light in his hand.

TWELVE

A RUNNING JOKE in my family, at my Ita's expense, is, "¿Ya, se te olvidó que tienes Mamá?" The statement, "What, you forgot you have a mother?" says a lot about the root of my family's communication skills. A group now consisting of four people—me, my mom, my sister, and Tío—has turned the phrase into a family saying. We repeat it when we haven't talked to someone in a couple days, "¿Ya, se te olvidó que tienes hermana? ¿hija?"

"Who's calling?" I asked.

We were watching a movie in my mom's cluttered bedroom. My small body, curled onto its side, completed the handle to her teapot. It was one of the few days she was off from work. Her creased worn Customs uniform was strewn on the vanity stool. Other clothes, clean, were stacked in messy, colorful small mounds on top of the dresser. The only hint there was a piece of furniture underneath the piles was the wooden center mirror that stood tall. It was a mirror she rarely used since she was almost always getting dressed for work. In uniform, she looked the same every day.

The night before, Mom had worked a graveyard shift. This morning, she'd called the school and told them I wasn't feeling well. The Fritos and Red Devil hot sauce I had just eaten sat heavy in my stomach. It was afternoon now, and we had our pajamas on.

"Ay, it's your Ita."

She glanced at the display on the black cordless phone and set it back down.

"¡Gorda! ¿Dónde estás? Háblame," Ita's voice crackled over the answering machine speaker.

I looked up at Mom. Ita had given her the nickname Gorda when she'd gotten pregnant with Angie, and it had stuck.

"I'll call her later," she said, turning back toward the TV.

I asked my family what they were like before I was born. I wanted to understand the family dynamic, specifically why Mom and Ita's relationship always seemed so complicated. When I asked each of them separately about our family, they said different, but similar, things. I think each of their versions is true in its own way.

My mom says: "Your tío always got away with everything, while I always got the brunt of it. I used to wash the dishes while standing on a chair, that's how young I was! I helped cook, clean up. Where was your uncle? He could do no wrong, and me, I had to bail your Ita out of her messes, like the time she 'forgot' to pay the property taxes on the house. Where was your tío then? And, you know your Ita: money just slipped through her fingers—"

Ta Taa Ta Taaaaa!

The familiar honk blared outside and echoed down the otherwise quiet block. Mom was here. I had to hurry.

"Bye, Ita!" I grabbed my backpack and Mom's mail that still came to Ita's address from when Mom, Angie, and Ita had lived together when I was a toddler.

"Ay, pero tengo unas cosas para tu Mamá."

My grandma always bought us little things. I think it was her way of showing affection. My mom does the same thing now. She'll call me out of the blue and asks me to run outside because she bought me a plant.

I looked at her and began to turn toward the door. "I'll tell Mom." I let the screen door slam behind me. Before stepping out onto the porch, I heard the honk again.

Ta Taa Ta Taaaaa!

"M
O
M!
I
T
A
H
A
S
S
O
M
E
T
H
I
N
G
S

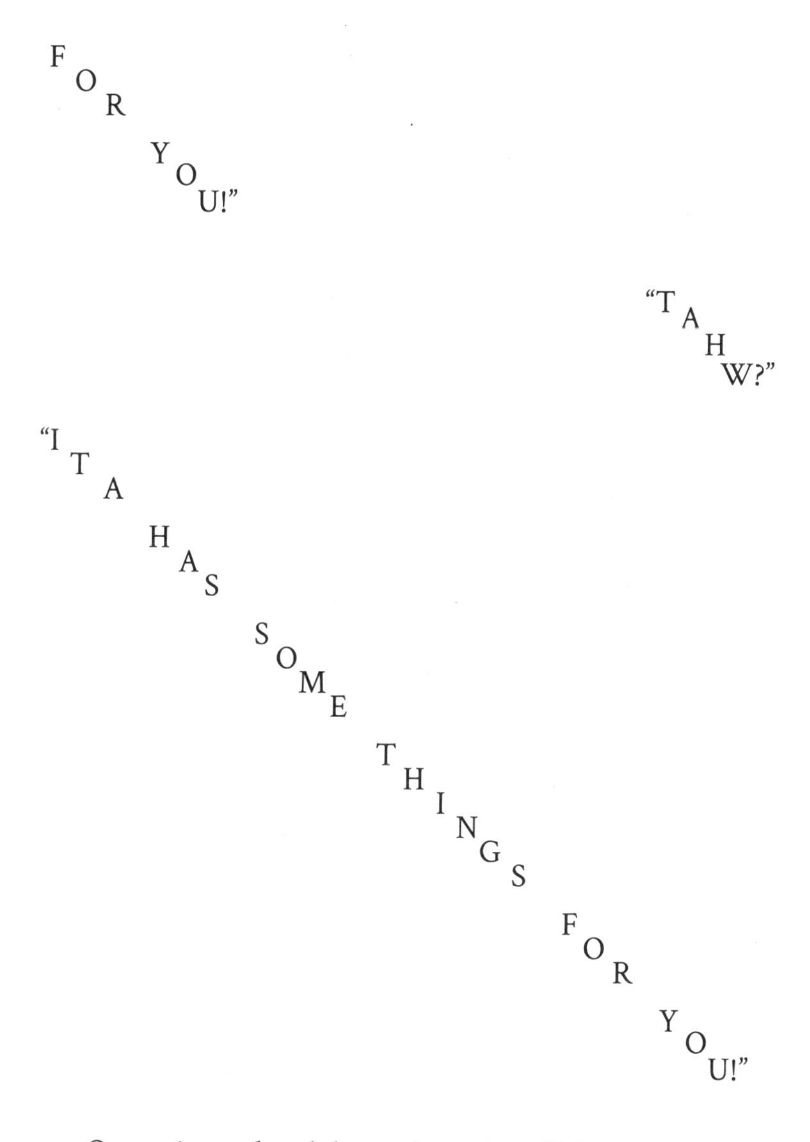

Our voices echoed down the stairs off the concrete and each porch on the block filled with brick Craftsman houses until it disappeared at the intersection of California Street and Brown. Mom paused, her brown Blazer idling in the street, and pushed at her hair.

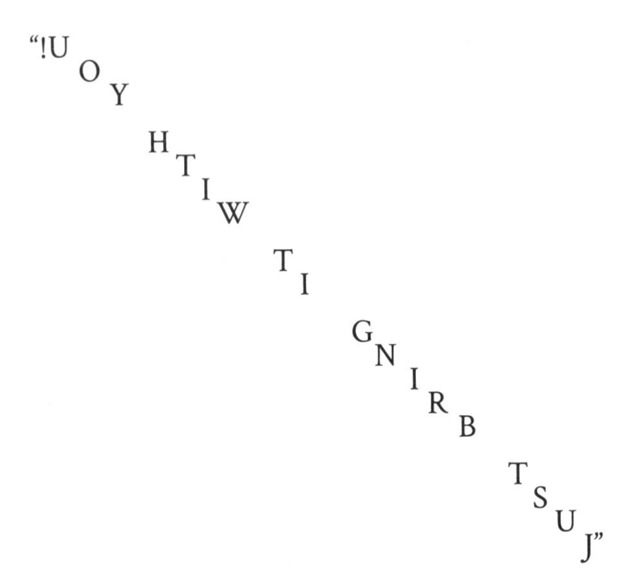

I glanced back at the shadowed screen door to see my grandma already bringing out a plastic bag in her hand.

"Le compré una blusa en el town. Dile que me hable, si le gustó."

I took the blouse she had gotten for Mom and listened as she made the same complaints she did every time this happened. Mom was always in a rush and didn't want to come up. I thought she was right because I also always had to rush out. Mom hardly came upstairs, and if I took too long, she scolded me once I got in the truck. I think my grandma always forgot that my mom was tired and just wanted to go home after work. I also think my mom forgot that Ita just missed her daughter. I wish I had realized it and pointed it out to both of them.

My tío says: "Your mom always took everything too seriously. You know how your mom can be uptight? She wasn't always like that. Before she married your dad, Moms helped her a lot with Angie and babysitting, just like she did with you. Your mom was just a kid when she had Angie, mija. Moms could have forced her to get married, but she didn't. Instead, she helped her. Your mom doesn't think about that. But you know your mom, just always has to prove everyone wrong, that she can do it on her own. She has to be right no matter what."

Mom's first love was named John. Johnny drove a 1969 yellow Super Sport that soon helped get him into trouble. In more ways than one.

It's an early spring weekend and Mom is driving. The window is open, and the breeze rustles her long parted dark hair. Tío is in the back seat. Two friends are with them. They all wear tight bell bottom jeans. The girls have on halter tops and snug t-shirts. Tío wears a button-down. His long shaggy hair rests on the shirt's wide collar. The '60s have just ended, and the age of disco will quickly engulf the radio waves. It was just supposed to be a regular night with a group of teens out cruising.

"Sis, isn't that Johnny's car?" Tío asks.

"Yeah, it is," she says.

The two friends look at Tío, then back at Mom, who has gone mute but keeps driving.

"Who's he with?" one of the friends asks.

Mom leans forward in her seat but can only make out the passenger's shape. It's a girl.

"I think you should follow him," Tío says. "Let's see who he's with."

Coming to a stop, Mom turns and sees Tío looking at her, eyebrow raised. The question he is asking doesn't need to be said aloud. Mom knows that eyebrow. She has it too. They both got it from Ita. It asks the tough questions wordlessly in the shape of its sharp arch. She nods, clenches her hands around the steering wheel, and follows Johnny onto the highway. When they end up on the outskirts of the city, a dead-end road behind a bowling alley, Mom quickly parks and all four of them try to hide, sliding down in their seats. Johnny parks further ahead. Tío's mouth is a thin line, and the friends are silent. The only sound is the low hum of Led Zeppelin's "Whole Lotta Love" that plays on the radio.

"Aren't you gonna go see?" Tío asks.

Mom shakes her head. She doesn't say anything because, if she does, her voice might crack. If she's learned anything from Ita, it's that she has to be strong. Tío and the friends look at each other but stay silent. They know what this dead-end road is all about.

When the windows on the Super Sport start to fog—so to speak—Tío reaches for the door, but Mom stops him.

"No."

She steps out of the car. Her friends watch her petite frame move in the darkness. The yellow car is rocking slightly. Mom knows this place. And she knows this rocking. When she reaches the car, she grabs the door handle, and it opens. Could she be that strong? But no, Johnny forgot to lock the car. He's with Silvia Ponce—her friend. It's here, Mom says, she learned she can't trust any man.

Weeks later, seventeen years old, Mom realizes she's pregnant. She's already told Johnny, and he promises things will be different, but she's not sure. She can't get the scene from the car out of her head.

After Mom broke the news, Ita surprised her. Mom is stunned. It's 1970, but Ita's openness to a pregnancy out of wedlock is surprising—especially for our culture, so traditional even today. "No eres la primera ni seras la última embarazo fuera del matrimonio. No tienes que casarte si no quieres," she says.

I imagine Ita, once the shock and anger have faded, sitting on the edge of Mom's bed. I see her as she holds Mom's hand and plays with her fingertips just a little as she tells her she doesn't have to marry Johnny if she doesn't want to. Tears slide down Mom's cheeks even though she wishes she weren't crying. Mom's jaw clenches and unclenches as she tries to swallow them back. The sound of Gil watching TV from the living room keeps the silence from becoming too heavy.

What is she going to do?

Ita thinks Mom should put Johnny to the test, see if he is the hombresito he should be.

Mom nods. Ita's suggestion sounds fair. It gives her a glimmer of hope even though Mom wipes at her cheek with the back of her hand and sniffs. She wants to lean into Ita to rest against her chest and cry all the tears she's been holding in, but instead, she pulls away from Ita and folds her hands into two small fists in her lap.

The next day she calls Johnny, tells him she needs money. "The doctor says I need a prescription. For the baby," she breathes into the phone.

Johnny has a job. He has to help, right? There is a long

pause on the other side of the phone, and Mom hopes that Ita's idea was a good one. That this will prove he's going to be there for her and the baby.

"I don't have it," he says. "Look, I gotta go. I have work."

Mom nods but doesn't say anything. She should have known better. After everything. She blinks away the sting in her eyes and sets her jaw. Her knuckles turn white around the phone. She still holds it to her ear even after the line clicks. It's here, Mom says, she learned the only person she can rely on is herself.

My sister Angie says: "Ita always took care of me like she did with you. I even remember when Ita worked for the chinos downtown: I would sit in a corner and play while Ita worked. I was with Ita all over the place just like you. Mom's just so hard on Ita, you know? She takes for granted that Ita wasn't obligated to help, but she always did. Ita took us everywhere and fed us, and when she could, she bought us things we wanted. Ita didn't have to do all that. Especially with you, Ita didn't work and just had her Social Security check and the apartments. Mom forgets all the things Ita did for her and focuses on stuff from twenty years ago that she didn't do. Mom resents the fact that Ita asked her for money for watching us, but that's how she fed us. She resented like what, $40 a week? Who else was Mom gonna get to take care of us like that? *Oh! Tío's her favorite. Oh! She wouldn't have that house if it wasn't for me! She wouldn't have this or that if it wasn't for me!* Mom doesn't stop to think what she *wouldn't* have without Ita."

When I ask Angie what Ita and Mom fought about, it always goes back to money. It was always money. They kept a running tally of who owed who what until the day she died. When I was five, Mom and Ita got into a fight about the babysitting money. Even though Mom supported both households, Ita asked for $40 a week to watch me. In retrospect, I think that $40 bought my small toys from the Newberry store downtown and cheeseburgers at the Hamburger Hut nearby. But finally my mom had enough, and she told Ita, "Forget it," and put me in daycare.

For a month, I went to a daycare just a few blocks from Ita's house. I only remember the icky heavy feeling I still get when I think about that place. My stomach clenches when I remember the forced naps on a hard-blue plastic coffin-shaped beds. I'd lift my head, and the caregiver would give me an evil eye until I lay back down. I didn't move, eyes open, until nap time was over. I didn't take naps when I was with Ita.

After a few sleepless afternoons, they let me go with a lady I liked. She took care of the babies, but since I wasn't a baby, I couldn't stay with her all day.

Once, she let me call Ita. The tan phone felt cool in my hot little hand.

"Hello?"

"Ita?" I whispered not to wake the babies.

"Prieta! ¿Qué le pasó?"

"Nothing, Ita. I'm okay," I paused swallowing back the sting in my throat. "But can you come get me from this place? I don't like it here."

I heard the sound of *General Hospital* in the background.

Our novela.

"I can't, Prieta. I'm sorry. Habla con tu mamá."

She sighed as the nice lady took the phone out of my hand. I had already told my mom I didn't like this place. Every day I told her, but she didn't listen.

When I ask Angie why Mom finally took me back to Ita's, she tells me, "You started losing your hair from the stress. You got a bald spot on the top of your head, and when Mom saw it, she freaked out and took you back to Ita."

"A bald spot?!"

"Yup," Angie nods.

I believe all the versions are true and overlap. I wasn't there to see my mom and Tío as children, but I was there to see how Ita babied my uncle and practically waited on him when we ate together. She served him his plate at the table while the rest of us got our own food. She saw him as the man of the house.

This Mexican tradition makes me cringe. It makes me wrinkle my nose at Ita because, as much as she went against the grain, she clung to this business about men.

Mom felt like she was second fiddle her whole life, just how Mamá Lupe treated Ita. Both never left their mother's side, even when they felt unloved. Even though Ita felt the brunt of Mamá Lupe's coldness, she seemed to carry some of that on to my mom. Ita was able to love Angie and me gentler, with more warmth.

Who knows why?

My mom was hard long before I came along. I think she had to be though: Ita, Johnny, and who knows who else. The job she took—in a male-dominated field founded on machismo, which she had to take from both her co-workers *and* the people making the daily commute over the international bridges between Juárez and El Paso—didn't help either. Mom was the provider. She didn't have a choice.

Ita, well, her life and all the different paths it took didn't seem to be any easier. Even harder, maybe. But with us, she was softer. Hugs and caresses. Chinese checkers and refried bean burritos. Maybe that's why—I'd like to believe—Angie and I are a little different.

"¿Ya, se te olvidó que tienes Mamá?" My mom's laugh crackled through the phone.

"*Ha ha,* hi, Mom," I forced the laughter.

"What are you doing, mija?"

"You know, working, Ita—I mean Mom," I poke.

"Sí, chistosita, it's because I haven't heard from you in days. Your Ita? She always exaggerated everything. I talked to her sometimes three times a day, and there she was, telling your uncle and your sister she hadn't talked to me. Se olvidaba nomás cuando le convenía a esa señora."

I rolled my eyes at my mom. *Sure, Mom: Only Ita forgot things when it was convenient.* Good thing Mom couldn't see my face.

THIRTEEN

ITA CALLED MOM *Gorda* for as long as I could remember. While my mom's weight fluctuated through the years, I've seen pictures of Mom when she was young, and she definitely wasn't gorda.

In one of those pictures, she's sitting in a round booth with Ita and Tío and wearing bell bottom jeans and a snug V-neck blouse. She has long brown hair parted down the middle. Her eyes, deep set, look dreamy and older than the baby face that holds them. It's my mom, but it isn't. She isn't anyone's mom yet. She is a girl who doesn't know that soon she'll be pregnant.

For now, she still smiles at the camera, small like she has a secret. There is a slight gap between her front teeth. The one I've heard stories about but never saw. Mom chipped her front tooth horse-playing with Tío when she was thirteen. A dentist in Juárez just pulled the other half out instead of capping it. Slowly the other teeth began to spread out until the missing tooth became a gap. When the girl in the picture became my mom, her teeth were already fixed. I never saw her gap.

Even though she's sitting, Mom looks small and compact.

She is bigger than Ita, fuller bosomed, but that's just because Ita was even more petite. Mom says that, in Ita's prime, she was a whopping five feet, two inches and a whole hundred and five pounds soaking wet. To me, Mom and Ita look larger than life, so late '60s retro cool—small packages that held a lot of punch.

Later, when Mom is older, she'll look at this same picture and tell me she remembers that this was just before she got pregnant with Angie. That's when Ita started calling her Gorda because of how her pregnant belly grew.

Ita called Angie *Güerinchi* when she was little. As she got older, she just became Güera. It's because she was light-skinned. Ita had fair skin too. My mom's, with just a splash of café, could also be called fair, but Angie got the nickname Güera because she had gringo fair skin from her dad Johnny.

When Angie was little, people thought she was Ita's daughter because they looked a lot alike. I think I can see it in her first Holy Communion picture. Angie looks somber. Her big brown eyes face the camera with a quiet curiosity that seems more adult than little girl.

When I was born, Angie was ten. She was so happy for me to arrive and tells me a story of watching over me from the baby observation window. I imagine the same big brown eyes from the photo peering in on me, but this time with a hint of a smile.

It's not until I'm older that I realize that technically we're half-sisters. But even though I'd noticed I was the only prieta in our family, Angie was always my whole sister, even when she was acting like a mom.

Ita called me Prieta. She called me this because my skin is a toasted brown. When I was born my mom says I was light-skinned, but she knew "que iba ser morena"—that I was going to be darker—because the insides of my little baby thighs were already darker than the rest of me.

In the sun, I turn a darker brown. I get even more prieta.

"Prieta" is a term of endearment. When I tell people who don't speak Spanish what "prieta" means—"dark" or the "dark one"—their eyes pop open and a small gasp escapes. I see the offense they feel for me sprinkled on their faces like the freckles I will never have.

How do I tell them that when I heard Ita say "Prieta," I felt the caress of her strong hands on the top of my head as she braided my hair? How do I tell them that I never knew what "Prieta" really meant until some light-skinned Mexican kids laughed at me and said I had to be more Mexican than them because I was "bien prieta"? How do I tell them that when they said the word, it turned ugly, and I called them wetbacks in response? How do I tell them that now, even after the cruelty of children, "Prieta" means love? That each time "Prieta" fell from her lips, I learned to love my dark skin.

No one calls me that anymore. I miss how her words sounded out loud.

My Ita called me Prieta. When she died, she took the name with her.

FOURTEEN

Seven

Seven: The number of things about Ita we never talk about.

"Seven," we say in low whispers even if we're sitting in the quiet of our living rooms. Someone might hear us.

Seven miscarriages, eight aunts and uncles, including my one uncle, who's alive.

"What happened?" I ask. "What was wrong?" But I don't get a response.

I think back to all those times Ita had that far away look in her eye. When she was with me, but she really wasn't. Now, I believe she was imagining what it would have been like if she had been able to have all eight children. After learning so much about her, I think I can see it and also the weight of the missed life. I imagine four aunts, four uncles, and my mom. Their names: Lucilla, Margarita, Josephina, Guadalupe, my mom Leticia, Antonio Jr., Alfredo, Francisco, and my tío Roberto, all similar in age, only a year or two apart.

Antonio Jr. lives in Denver. Josephina and Margarita live in Los Angeles. My mom, Tío Roberto, Guadalupe,

Lucilla, and Francisco all stay in El Paso. Alfredo lives in Houston. We'd have a family reunion every year, and they would all come back to El Paso with cousins and wives and husbands. Just like Ita, I've imagined their whole lives.

Tía Josephina, a lesbian, brings her partner Mia and stepdaughter Jessica. Tía José is beautiful, curly dark hair and light-brown almond eyes which glow against her brown skin. My Ita says, "Pero està tan bonita, no sé qué le pasó a mija"—as if something had to happen to make her gay. We treat Jessica like our cousin, even though she isn't really, unless she gets a snotty attitude about being from L.A. Then we just ignore her. We try not to giggle later when she gets pregnant at sixteen. "*Oooo,* but I'm from L.A.," I say to my cousin Lucy, Tía Lucilla's daughter.

Tía Lucilla has Lucy and Mario. Lucy is my closest cousin because we grew up together.

My mom and Tía Lucilla are also the closest because they were pregnant with us at the same time. She is going through a hard time right now, her eyes always shiny, on the verge of tears, because she divorced Uncle Paco last year after being married for twenty years. My mom jokes and says, "Qué aguante." She always thought Uncle Paco wasn't good enough for Tía Lucy. My mom is just like that though. Even if they're the best people, well-off, loving, romantic, they're never good enough for her brothers and sisters.

Tía Rita—we call her that because the name *Margarita* is too long—has three kids: Marco, Alberto, and Antonio. Marco and Antonio are cool and have good jobs. Marco is a bus driver and Antonio owns a dry cleaning business. They both help Tía Rita, unlike Alberto. He got into trouble when we were all younger and is in jail for drugs. We don't talk about that though. It was very hard on Tía Rita, and her hair went from jet black to a wiry silver-gray in a year. Now she dyes it, but it looks harsh against her pale skin, highlighting the hollows of the heartache Alberto put there.

Tía Lupe—we call her that because Guadalupe sounds like a viejita name—has one son, Hector David. We have to call him by his full name too. No, "Hey, Hector," or "Hey, David." Nope. He gets a crazy twitch in his eye, then sighs so loud you'd think he was holding in one of the gusts from the spring El Paso dust storms. Tía Lupe is the quiet one in the family. Silent. Judging. If she wasn't my aunt, I'm not sure we'd like her. She's stern and very regañona. Always scolding or getting ready to scold. While Hector David sighs gusts of hot desert air, Tía Lupe's lips release the words that sting like the grains of sand in that gust. Ita says maybe she shouldn't have named her after her mother Mamá Lupe, since she didn't seem to appreciate it anyway. Ita spent her whole life trying to win Mamá Lupe over and even named one of her daughters after her, y nada. Tía Lupe ended up salty, just like Mamá Lupe. Pobre.

Tío Paco, not the *Uncle* Paco that married into the family but *our* Tío Paco, has been married three times. We joke and tell him the fourth time is a charm because of Ita and Tony, the fourth husband that stuck. We say Tío Paco is a mujeriego, a womanizer, because he has six kids, two from each wife. I've seen old black and white pictures of him. He was handsome. Now, he's softened in the jaw, the skin hanging just a little like a balloon losing its air. Some of his kids—like Terry, the oldest, and Frank Jr., from his second wife—come to the family reunions and visit Ita often. But the others don't. They hate their dad, and although I can understand—because my own dad wasn't around either—I still love my Tío Paco. They look the most like him out of all of his kids though: dark hair, brown eyes, light skin. I wonder if they hate a little bit of themselves too, just like I did.

Tío Prieto—that's what we call Alfredo because he's dark, dark like a cocoa bean—lives in Houston with his high school sweetheart. He is the only one of the siblings who hasn't gotten divorced and has been married since he was twenty. He has two kids: James and Mercedes. They don't really speak any Spanish. The rest of us at least understand, but they think they are gringos even though they are as dark as Tío Prieto. Ita says, "Ay, si, muy gringos con el culo prieto." Skin gets browner in certain places, brown arm, browner ass crack. Latinos with fair skin can't hide their heritage, and Ita was always quick to point it out. We laugh at them behind their backs and imitate the way they say things like *tort-til-las* and *tah-cos* when they aren't around. Marco will say, "Who am I? Who am I? Can we have *Tah-cos* for dinner?" and the cousins all laugh. Tío Prieto gets mad at us, but he smiles while he does it, so I think he laughs too.

Tío Tony Jr. works for the FBI and doesn't talk much about his work. It's top secret. He's always in black slacks and tucked-in polo shirts, sporting aviators, even on Sundays. He is the youngest of the brothers and sisters and lives in Denver.

When Ita met Tony, he was a paratrooper. In their wedding picture, he's tall. Because he towers over Ita in her powder blue dress suit, she looks even smaller than she is. My mom and Tío Roberto were six and seven years old when Ita married him. I imagine Tony as kind and understanding even though only four of the kids were really his. He was a dad to everyone. He had to be because Ita always said Tony was the love of her life.

Thc family reunions are filled with music from Chente and Amalia Mendoza, Juanga, and oldies from the aunts and uncles' youth. We explain Spotify to Tío Paco every reunion, but he still makes comments like, "Wow, this is a good station! Can you record these songs for me?" The house overflows with laughter, so much food, lots of drinks, and the clinks and clanks of dishes. Someone is always washing dishes. Each branch of the family cooks a different plate for the reunion. Tacos de carne molida and asada, red enchiladas, rice, beans, ribs from the grill, macaroni salad. Store-bought sandwiches that Tía José brings because she can't cook (she fried an egg and left a big black greasy stain on Ita's yellow kitchen wall), mole and fried chicken. We also make trips to Chico's Tacos and Good Luck Café. El Paso classics. They'd never visit El Paso without eating Good Luck tacos.

The smaller ones that are starting to appear—Mica, Ale, Carlos, and Temo—yell and scream while they play or cry and run to one of the many moms in the house when something goes wrong. Ale, my niece, runs to my sister Angie the most. "Mom, they hurt my feelings," she says, tears streaming down her cheeks, her mouth so squished the words come out like mushed baby food.

If a new boyfriend or girlfriend comes, sometimes they

leave after falling asleep on the sofa—or worse, leave early because we are all too much for them, the noise, the jokes. When they leave, Ita calls them "desabridos," and no fun, and she and Tony laugh as she puts her hand on his thinning leg. Desabridos means tasteless. Ita means they don't have zest and not in the English classless kind of way. In the "they don't have flavor," sazón, sabor, personality, that energy that attracts people. See? Desabridos just works way better here, and the gringos don't understand the word which makes it better. One time, a girlfriend thought Ita said desebrada and said she loved those types of *tah-cos.* We all turned like *to-mah-tes* from holding in the carcajadas. I imagine them laughing at jokes like this from the very beginning of their marriage, fifty years ago, if they were still alive today.

We spend the first weekend in May together before it gets too hot in El Paso, eating and drinking, talking and dancing, listening to Chente and Javier, our voices mingling to make music unique to our family, a symphony of English and Spanish, accents, jokes, stories, and laughter. I make the Bloody Marys for the tíos and tías in the morning. Ita and Tony, when the whole family is together, joke and poke at each other like two teenagers. She'd always wanted love and a big family to fill her house with noise and laughter.

My throat aches here, like when Ita sang those sad songs. She'd always wanted love and a big family to fill her house with noise and laughter, but no matter how hard she tried, it didn't happen. Instead of eight aunts and uncles, it's just my mom, my Tío Roberto, Angie, and me. A small family, a quarter of the one that could have been. Ita's house was quiet and filled with the echo of telenovelas and an infrequently ringing phone.

"But Mom—seven miscarriages?"

"No, just one. Tony's baby. My mom, well, she wasn't the same after that."

"I guess we're lucky that you and Tío were already born then, huh? But the others? What do you mean, not the same?"

"You know that last baby, your grandma wanted it so badly. She was married to Tony then—"

"Her fourth husband, right?"

"Yes, Tony, she loved him. She always said that he was *el amor de su vida.* I think that's why she was happy she could finally have the baby, but it was an ectopic pregnancy, and she almost died. She always said that Diosito had punished her for all the others because this one she'd wanted the most."

"What do you mean punished?"

"Ay, mija, it was the fifties, and your grandma worked two jobs, a line supervisor in a textile factory, before she hurt her back. Random jobs until she tended bar at the Azteca, right there off Stanton Street at night, just to support your uncle and me. She wouldn't have been able to support all of us. No one knew about birth control then. She did what she had to do, and went to Juárez, *para que la curaran.*"

Mom's words echo, *so they could cure her,* and I feel the weight of this imagined life, too. Now, I can see how the guilt of impossible situations slowly broke Ita down, and I wonder if the lifelong mourning isn't what really took her from us.

FIFTEEN

THE HEAT WAS suffocating, inescapable. Ita and I sat in the living room watching the evening news with the front door open to capture whatever breeze might pass by—we could at least dream there would be a breeze in this dry desert. The stars twinkled behind the large screen door, making it seem like a window to the outside. It was scary and wonderful sitting there by the dim lamplight.

When the news ended, we got ready for bed. I put on my cotton nightgown and sat, waiting as my grandma performed her nightly ritual. The red-brick house, built in 1920 in a row with similar houses, on blocks unfolding down the sloped end of the Rocky Mountains, was so old the rooms didn't have light switches. There was only a single light bulb hanging from the ceiling in the middle of the room and it kept us safe from the dark.

I sat in bed, legs stretched out and crossed, watching Ita as she took off her makeup. She used cold cream and a pair of men's old and threadbare underwear, which was covered with black smudges of mascara and eyeliner, and colored tinges from the many eye shadows she wore. She wiped at her face until it glistened as if she'd used the old underwear to polish it. I wondered who those calzones had belonged to but never asked. I liked to imagine they were Tony's, my favorite of all her husbands.

The Mexican radio station played fuzzily in the background. I stared out the window and into the blackness. The window's thick wooden frame was another portal into the unknown. The only safe place was sitting here, watching Ita.

She sat on the edge of the bed and rubbed thick white Nivea cream in a circular motion on her feet. She complained about the bunions she was sure would appear from the high heels she liked to wear. Boleros came on, as if on cue. Raw voices sang songs with more emotion than I could comprehend. Ita sat and hummed in a soft, rich voice that always bewitched me. She tilted her head back, a sad look in her shiny eyes.

Who was she thinking of? Whoever had put that look there had come and gone long ago.

Sometimes she talked a little, telling me about the Bible and how faith in God was what would keep bad things away from us. I said my Hail Marys to her in English, and she said El Credo in Spanish. After we were done, she put out the single beacon of light. The buzz and breeze from the fan, turning back and forth, lulled me to sleep as I lay in the dark, curling toward my grandma.

PART TWO

FINDING YASMÍN

SIXTEEN

I WANT TO tell you that things didn't change. That I didn't change. That I stayed with Ita until the very end. I want to tell you that when puberty hit, I didn't distance myself from my Ita and Mom. I want to tell you that Angie didn't kind of hate me and look at me with a perpetual judging eyeroll when she was in my vicinity. I want to tell you that I didn't start wearing flannel and raccooning my eyes with charcoal eyeliner by the time I got to eighth grade. I want to tell you that I didn't gain a permanent sneer for everyone and everything other than my skateboarding, pot-smoking, Nirvana-loving friends.

But then, I would be lying.

When I was old enough to stay by myself, I was at Ita's less and less. I disappeared into my books and music. Mom worked and Angie lived with her boyfriend, so I was on my own a lot. In the era of the latchkey kid, I thought that's what I wanted, but really, I think I just wanted them to notice me.

I remember reading a story—said to be an old Cherokee legend—in one of my books: a grandfather is teaching his grandson about the two wolves who battle inside of us. One is evil, and one is good. When the grandson asks who wins, the grandfather replies, "The one you feed."

The times I was left waiting for my dad did something to me. They flipped a switch in my head—or maybe something had already been brewing for a while, maybe since the day I fell and hit my head and he left the hospital before I was released. He never tried the way I imagined a father who loved his daughter would try.

I don't know. One day I just woke up hating the world. That didn't stop for a long time. My mom, Ita, Angie—even later my tío—were included in that hate.

I just kept feeding the wrong wolf.

SEVENTEEN

A Portion of the Large Intestine

Ita was sixty-two when she had surgery to remove a section of her large intestine. It had perforated. It wasn't an easy surgery. Mom was afraid Ita would die. I'd never seen Mom look like that. It was like she was angry, but her face was pale, and fear—not anger—clouded her eyes. At the hospital, Ita seemed so frail. It was the first time she looked like a viejita to me.

I was thirteen when this surgery happened. Mom and I moved in with Ita to take care of her. Mom packed her navy uniforms. I packed my black t-shirts and Nirvana CDs from our house on the Eastside of El Paso and moved into the home I'd loved so much as a child. Only now, I resented the whole situation with every inch of my being. My fears for Ita at the hospital evaporated the more the move became real. My ever-present sneer took its place. Adults were the enemy, and, even though I loved Ita, I didn't want to live with her.

As Ita healed and got better and better, the friction between my mom and her got worse. I didn't help. At first, they let me live in a bedroom on the second floor of the house. That quickly ended when Ita found a boy hiding in my closet. The yelling and the screaming are a tangle of shadows and noise in my memory.

"Alejate de mí antes de que te golpee, Yasmín!" Ita bellowed, hands fisted at her sides.

She was so angry, she used my name. I wasn't Prieta anymore. I fell to my knees in her blue bedroom, my hands steepled as I begged her not to tell my mom. I could see in her eyes that she thought about it. For a minute, she didn't see the sneering, indignant teen I'd become, but the little girl, her Prieta, twirling in her Sesame Street nightgown during Saturday morning cartoons.

"Nothing happened, Ita! I swear!" I pleaded with her. "Hit me! Give me golpes! Please! But don't tell my mom!"

As quickly as the look came, it vanished. Her jaw clenched, and she picked up the phone. I knew my world was crumbling away fast.

"Leticia, no te quería decir esto—"

I ran out of the house. It was nighttime, pitch black. I tried to take the steps as fast as I could without falling. I ran to the left, then stopped and looked up and down the block. Where should I go? My heart pounded in my ears. I wondered how Ita had finished the rest of that sentence. I imagined my mom's face. The night was quiet, and my breathing sounded loud and ragged as I ran the two blocks down to Arizona Street where my sister lived. I don't know what I thought would happen. I hoped that even though I'd shut Angie out of my life—just like I had my mom and Ita—that she could save me.

She couldn't.

My mom flew through Angie's front door before I could

even explain. As soon as I peered up from the couch and saw her coming, I locked my arms around my legs and folded into myself. My mom was pure white-hot rage. Her hands slammed down on my back and pummeled me. Loud thuds of her palms and sides of her fists thumped against my body. She tried to pull my hair, to slap my face, but I wouldn't budge. She hit my back over and over. I clutched my legs with a vise grip, but my muffled grunts and gulps for air filled the quiet living room.

"*Mom! Stop! Mom!*" Angie finally yelled from the corner of the room.

At the sound of her voice, I glanced up and saw her step forward. Her arms reached out, but she didn't get any closer. My mom's chest still heaved up and down. I pushed my face into my thighs and let out a deep wail.

I was put on full lockdown. No phone. I couldn't go anywhere or even glance in a direction I wasn't told to look. I had to share a bedroom with my mom. That same night, I lay next to my mom, hovering as close to the edge of the queen-sized bed as I humanly could. My cheeks burned as I gritted my teeth together. Her blows still stung.

The next day, my sister took me to get a pregnancy test at a local clinic. Her eyes were downcast, her face as pale as mine. She tried her best to talk to me, but I avoided her gaze and stared at anything that wasn't her. I retreated further into myself. The only thing I had left were the ever-present horror novels that I already used as an escape: R.L. Stine, John Saul, and Anne Rice books. No matter how angry I made my mom, she'd never take my books away.

Mom didn't know how to deal with me. Ita searched

my face for the little girl who'd once loved to cuddle and hug her, but she couldn't find her. I was so angry and I felt misunderstood. I didn't have the words to tell them I felt as if I didn't matter.

Even when my mom took me to a counselor for help, I sat behind a book for the first couple of sessions, refusing to speak.

I felt more alone than ever, but still the knot of anger in my belly spread. I could barely swallow sometimes. It grew piece by piece until it was an unbreakable armor that didn't break. It just hardened.

The Left Breast

Ita was sixty-three when she fell outside the house. We knew she was feeling better because she'd gone out for the first time since we'd moved in. I was sleeping with my mom in the front bedroom of Ita's house. The window was open to let in the chilly night breeze when we heard a soft yell, "Leticia!"

My mom woke up,."¿'Ora qué?"

I sat up, rubbing the sleep from my eyes. I peered at the clock: 1:15 a.m. *What now?* I ran outside. Mom was yelling at Ita, who was splayed out awkwardly on the landing at the top of the steps.

I helped Mom lift my grandma. Ita was covered in something red, something that smelled like tomato. She had fallen carrying a glass bottle of Clamato. The glass had broken against her chest. Once we got her inside, I saw a deep slice close to the top of the soft skin of her left breast. The red stains were Clamato mixed with blood.

My mom grunted and yelled as we sat Ita on the bathroom toilet seat. Then she stomped down the hallway to get dressed. "Qué estaba haciendo, Amá?" she yelled on her way to her bedroom. I'm not sure it mattered what Ita was doing when she fell. But my mom always lost her temper when we got hurt. She was always so quick to anger. The worry was often so mixed with it we couldn't tell the difference. All Mom saw was red.

I took off Ita's drenched blouse and bra and wiped what I could away. She held a towel against her boob to slow the bleeding. "I'm stupid, hu?" Ita slurred. She looked down at herself, gray pants and silver high heels covered in tomato-y blood. "Tenía que ser la chichi buena." I shrugged. Of course, it had to be the good boob. Later I pointed out things could have been much worse if it had been on the other side.

My mom walked back and forth from the bedroom to the bathroom to yell at my grandma and ask if she was okay.

I finally had to urge her, in a steady voice, to get dressed so we could take Ita to Southwestern General.

What happened, the doctor wanted to know. I stood next to Ita while my mom finished filling out paperwork. "I fell, doctor, and I have to be honest. I've been drinking since three in the afternoon," my Ita replied, her voice too loud for the quiet room. The doctor looked at me. I shrugged, hands in the air. Ita left with eight stitches and a stern talking-to.

When we got home, Mom helped Ita bathe as best she could in the claw-footed tub. In the dawn, while the light shifted from purple to orange, I sprayed the red stain on the landing and the stairs with the water hose, trying to wash away the bloody tomato juice.

My sister says she doesn't drink because of things like this. I'm not sure what happened to me.

The Rest of the Large Intestine

Three years later, at sixty-four, Ita was back in the hospital. Her whole large intestine needed to be removed. The new scar would run vertically from just below her belly button to disappear beneath her underwear.

This time, I stayed with Ita because my mom had been sent to a four-week training out of state for work. Mandatory can't-leave kind of training. This would happen twice that school year. Angie now lived in Dallas with her boyfriend Gabe. I had just turned sixteen. My angry boil had simmered. Weekly sessions with the counselor had helped channel it better. I read more. I scribbled in journals. And for all the stupid things I did? I was learning to look in the mirror even while I still made mistakes.

Ita looked older now. Her once plump cheeks were sunken and sallow. A sticky fear spread through my body. Even though both Angie and Mom called daily, I had to be an adult for the first time. I don't know where my tío was then. When we try to remember, we can't. Mom thinks he visited once. So—I was on my own. A few years before, all I had wanted was for them to leave me alone so I could do whatever the fuck I wanted. Now I was seeing that being an adult was not running and hiding to let someone else deal with the problem. It was staying when no one else could.

So—I went to school. After class, I picked up barbacoa tacos at Taco Tote near the hospital and stayed with Ita until visiting hours were over. Then I drove to Ita's to feed her dog Oso, a big fluffy chow, and bring in the mail, then to the Eastside to feed our dog Bear, a black Doberman, and check the mail. I forged my mom's signature on checks to pay any bills. Then I showered, went to bed, and got up just to do it again that day. The hospital stay was only a week, but in my memory, it was endless. The time outside of the hospital disappears somewhere in my mind.

EIGHTEEN

I went through phases when I wanted to see my dad, when I thought, "This time will be different." The memories before I was a teen are fragmented. Jumbled. I try to make sense of them, but each time I reach out for one, it slips just out of my grasp. If someone asked me how many times he stood me up, I wouldn't have an answer. It could have been three, or it could have been ten. It didn't matter how many times it was because what I do remember is the waiting. Worse, the fucking *hoping.*

One clear memory, when I was thirteen and Mom and I were living with Ita, is burned hard in my psyche. It was after Ita had found that boy in my room. I was still on lockdown, but the initial anger—bitter and smoky like charred chile de arbol left on the burner—no longer choked us. There had been symptoms of what my dad's disappearance had done to me before that boy, but it wasn't until after him that Mom realized I needed professional help. It seemed the emotional scars I caused us were worse than the pink dots sprinkled on Ita's stomach. I pretended I couldn't see the way Mom looked at me. She couldn't understand what was happening.

Her happy little girl had changed, and I was now a stranger to her.

I still wasn't allowed to use the phone or go anywhere on my own, but a visit to my dad's was permitted. I should have known better, though. The sinking feeling started while I got ready. I kept shooing it away, but like a fly on a hot summer day, it kept buzzing back.

I stood in the bathroom in baggy Goodwill Wranglers and a faded black t-shirt. I seemed harsh and out of place against the pink background that still held its herbal scent from Ita's bath earlier. I'd locked the bathroom door so they couldn't come in. I knew there was a limited amount of time before one of them tried, though. Locked doors were definitely not allowed. My outfit might have appeared scruffy, but I took a long time with my face and hair.

I smoothed powder a shade lighter than my skin over my face. The times I'd been made fun of for my dark skin as a kid still lingered. "Bien prieta!" the voices echoed, but anything lighter and it would be obvious. My insides yearned to be as white and thin as heroin chic model Kate Moss, whose face seemed to be in every magazine in the '90s. I gazed at her gaunt face, eyes rimmed with smudgy black makeup, lips stained red, and wished my body could be just as emaciated with pointy sharp angles. Having only a Coke for lunch helped a little, but no amount of not eating would ever get rid of my curved hips. The grunge era's androgyny was hard on a brown girl like me. I'd worn a C cup since the sixth grade, literally the antithesis of Kate Moss.

Even though I resembled my dad and his side of the family—dark eyes, black hair, brown skin—I hoped that if I looked just right, if he could just see me, he'd be my dad too, just like he was to my half-siblings. I'd finally have a real dad who wanted *me*.

I lined my inner eyelid and top lid with the blackest black charcoal liner, then layered on mascara. My hair, now chin-length, was parted down the middle and perfectly straight. I sprinkled baby oil into my hands, rubbed, and ran my fingers through my clean hair to make it shiny, piece-y, a little grungier. Staring in the mirror, I tilted my head from left to right and smoothed my hands over my hair again.

Since I was eleven, I'd begged my mother to let me get my hair cut. She finally let me. It was done in stages. Angie was in beauty school, and, while there were many trials and errors, I willingly sacrificed myself as her guinea pig. First, she cut the long dark hair that hung past my waist to the middle of my back. Mom took pictures and walked in and out of the kitchen crying.

A short time later, Angie cut it to my shoulders. I sighed with relief. The next day, I walked into my seventh-grade class feeling like the Vidal Sassoon commercials. I kept trying to flip my newly cut hair away from my face like the girls on TV.

Then the first boy said it, "You look like La Toya Jackson!"

He cackled. Then a handful of others did as well. As the class filled, the joke spread. I knew he'd said it because of my brown skin. Because I was dark. My hair wasn't curly, but there was *sooooo* much of it, it just poofed out. Angie hadn't cut it into layers. She'd just bluntly cut my bushy lion's mane. My best friend, Mia, told them to shut up, but it was already out there.

The length didn't last long. I begged. More.

"Shorter, Mom. Please."

Angie helped. "She already cut it, Mom. I mean, it's her hair."

Both Ita and Mom stared at my hair and tsked. "Pero tenías el cabello tan bonito," they said. I just rolled my eyes. Pretty to who? By eighth grade, my hair was a layered chin-length bob. It stayed that way for several years.

Now, standing in Ita's bathroom, I glared in the mirror and scoffed. The idea of girls having long hair was so *Mexican.* I heard Mom and Ita's comments about my long hair. I thought of my dad's family. I wanted nothing to do with that traditional image. I jutted my chin out and walked out of the bathroom.

I looked at the clock. I was thirty minutes early. *He was coming this time. My father.* I lay on my mom's bed, blue Vans hanging off the edge of it, and watched Green Day's "Basket Case" video for the umpteenth time. I felt like the band in the video, trapped in a mental institution, only allowed to play music when the staff let them. I didn't play anything, but my home now felt like a prison. Everything I did was supervised. The only difference was I wasn't medicated like them.

Mom was off today so she kept coming in and out of the room. I glanced from her face to the red numbers on the black alarm clock on her cluttered nightstand. Her eyes seemed to dart to the time more than mine. Her face reflected what I was thinking, but for some reason, I resented it. I focused on Billy Joe and the weird fat-faced masks on the TV instead.

When it was time for my dad to get there, I hovered

in front of the screen door. Only in the winter and during spring dust storms did Ita have the big wooden front door closed. I stood in front of my latched screen exit, checked my pockets to make sure I had my lip gloss, went back to the bathroom to check my hair, then back to look out the screen door to see if his blue Monte Carlo was at the bottom of the steps. I glanced at the clock again. Two minutes late. *He was coming this time. He had to, right?*

Last time, I'd called after he was supposed to come for me. There were voices and music in the background, and he said he'd mixed up the weekends.

When he was five minutes late, I went out to sit on the first step of the cement porch. My mom was silent, but her eyes still darted, and I didn't want her to watch me fidgeting back and forth between the bathroom mirror and the screen door. Outside, at least I would see him as he drove to stop in the middle of the block.

The sun was out, but I sat in the porch shade. Only the tips of my Vans were touched by the sun. I know it wasn't summer or else I would have never ventured out into the stifling heat. Sweat would have sprung along the bridge of my nose and upper lip, ruining the matte powder I'd smoothed over my face. It must have been springtime—the small window after the spring desert sandstorms and before the initial summer heat came in mid-May.

I tugged at the curled cuff of my jeans. I'd cut little one-inch slits on each of the side seams, so they'd fall over my shoes instead of bunching at my ankle, but each time I smoothed it down, the blue jean edge curled right back up. I crossed my legs, re-crossed them. No matter what, the block was still empty. When I heard a noise on the street, I leaned forward, eyes searching for a blue car, but—no—it was just an old gold car. I sat back, palms flat against the ground.

"Mija, should I call him?"

Mom's voice came through the screen door. I turned around. Her face was barely visible through the black mesh of the screen.

"No. It's okay."

I faced the street again, stared at the rows of houses. They were all similar to Ita's. Long rows of stairs leading up to a porch. Some had potted plants on cement slabs framing the porch or attempts at grass on the sloped lawns. Others, like Ita's, just had rocky dirt with patches of crabgrass.

I don't know how much time passed, but I didn't want to go inside. My butt felt flat and had gone numb a while ago. I shifted, but the grainy ground was unforgiving. I didn't want to see my mom's face or Ita's. I didn't want them to see my face. If Mom peered at me, brows furrowed in the center, I would scream. I didn't need her pity. I didn't need anyone's pity.

The screen door slammed. Mom came striding out, handbag in hand.

"Come on, mija. Let's go to the mall," she said, smile tight.

"*The mall?*"

I didn't move.

"I need to get some things, and didn't you want to look at some new tennies?"

I still didn't move. She came closer, "Vente, mija." She nudged at my arm with her knee.

I hesitated. Opened my mouth to say something, but

for once I didn't have any words. I trailed behind her on the stairs. The tears I'd been holding in escaped. I rubbed at my cheeks with the back of my hand and tried to slow my breathing. I brushed at my face, trying to hide them, but Mom knew.

I stared out the passenger window. I didn't want to look at her. I couldn't bear it if I saw her look at me like *that.*

Music low in the background helped ease the silence. When we got to the Cotton and Montana intersection, the light turned red. Mom put her hand on my thigh, warm, and squeezed gently. It was just a second, but almost instantly my chest heaved and the resolve I'd made on the porch, jaw clenched, dissolved as tears fell from my cheeks. I stared into my lap, still unable to meet her eyes, but this time for a different reason.

The light turned green. She lifted her hand from my leg to move the gear shift. The rest of the way to the mall, I sniffed silently and stared as the El Paso skyline smeared into colors of blue and gray.

NINETEEN

A WHILE AFTER being stood up by my dad, Mom and I were going somewhere, when she pointed, "Mira, mija."

I looked up to see a sign that said "Free Kittens" posted in someone's yard. She had already started to slow.

"Let's look."

I didn't really want to look at the kittens. Ita didn't like cats. She was old-Catholic-lady-weird about them. She thought they were evil. But Mom parked anyway. On the lawn, a blond woman and her kid sat on lawn chairs, while a dark-haired man and a little girl peered in the box.

"This one, Dad! I love this one. He's going to be my Snowball, because he's white like snow," the little girl giggled.

I frowned and rolled my eyes. Snowball? What a stupid name.

My mom caught the look on my face out of the corner of her eye and gave me a warning glance.

In the cardboard box, there were still four kittens. One of them was off to the side by herself. She seemed scrawny, tiny compared to the others.

"How old are they?" Mom asked.

The blond woman shaded her eyes with her hand. "Just

turned nine weeks, so they're ready for their new home."

I knelt and put my hand into the box as Mom chatted with the woman. Just then, the blond lady's kid stood and peeked in the box with me.

"You see that one?" She pointed at the tiny kitten by herself in the corner. "Mom says that's the runt. That's why she's so small. Sadie, her mother, didn't love her that much—"

"Now, Lauren, that's not what that means," her mom interrupted. "It just means she's special." She winked at me.

I frowned and glanced back down into the box. The "runt" didn't approach me. I moved my hand closer to her, and she sniffed. Her eyes were bright green.

"She's cute, no, mija?"

"Yeah, but what about Ita? Won't she say something?" I asked.

"*¿YYYY?*" Mom dragged out the one syllable.

I shrugged. The kitten was pretty scrawny, but I nodded and moved to pick her up.

"Mom, look." I held my left palm out. "She fits in my hand."

The teeny kitten sniffed my palm and let out the tiniest meow.

"Do you want her, mija? Let's take her," Mom said, without waiting for me to respond.

"But," I hesitated, "are you sure? What about Ita?" I asked again.

Mom shrugged. "She'll just have to deal with it. ¿Y si no? Pues ni modo. You like her, don't you?"

"Yeah," I hesitated.

She was kind of cute. Ita was not going to like Mom's

"deal with it" attitude, but that actually made the gray furball kind of cuter. I'd finally have something that was mine, and Mom had already made up her mind. There was no changing it after that.

Ita was not happy when we got home later that day with a litter box, cat food, and the tiny kitten I had named Drew, after Drew Barrymore, clinging to my shirt.

"Yo no quiero gatos en mi casa," she bellowed.

I moved into the bedroom I shared with Mom so Ita's voice wouldn't scare Drew.

"Pues qué bueno que no es solo su casa," Mom retorted.

Uh-oh. This was going to be one of those kinds of arguments where Mom reminded Ita that she had paid for the house. I quietly closed the door, so it was opened just a crack and I wouldn't have to hear Mom and Ita. I didn't want to be any part of the argument. I lay down on the bed with Drew. She was on her back, and I tickled her teeny belly and quickly snapped my hand back as her four little legs wiggled to catch me.

"I'm gonna love you and take you everywhere, Drew B. You're gonna be a badass cat. You got it?"

In my memory, she meows back in response. Her way of saying "Hell yeah!" Little did I know that tiny runt would be my constant companion for a long time.

TWENTY

I HAD A plan when I started high school: Go to summer school. Graduate in three years. Leave El Paso. Flip the city off as I leave. Go to Seattle. Go to college. Never come back.

Only three of those things happened.

The summer before my freshman year, I went to summer school. At first, my mom was suspicious. She had a firm report card rule. Nothing below a B—so she knew I didn't *have* to go. And really, who wants to go to summer school? But I convinced her there were no ulterior motives, and there weren't. Really.

Lucky for me, that year's sessions were at the oldest school in the city, El Paso High. They call her the Lady on the Hill. Indeed, she sits like a Roman goddess on a mountainside at the base of the Franklins. It was where I'd yearned to go since kindergarten, when I thought I was going to school with Angie. Angie went there and so did my mom and my uncle. And now I was going there too. It was one of the few family traditions I didn't turn my back on.

We were still living with Ita. Each morning, I walked up to la High, leaving early to avoid the heat. The indigo morning glories I passed along the way were already beginning to close, it was so hot. This meant that sweat appeared along the bridge of my nose.

First thing, I'd head to the bathroom to blot and re-powder my face, then to class. The room was filled with Mexican kids who had just moved to this side of the river to go to school, cholos with Sauvecito slicked-back hair and sagging Dickies, and a girl with fire red hair who smiled and introduced herself as Jennifer the Slut. I didn't tell anyone why I was there. No one asked. They all assumed I needed summer school. I was going to keep my head down, pass Geography I and II, and start the year with two credits checked off.

That's what I was going to do.

Until I saw a boy who I thought looked like Ethan Hawke from *Reality Bites.* My favorite movie. Maybe he didn't really look like Ethan except that he was a couple years older than me, tall, white, and blue-eyed. Truthfully, he caught my eye because he was a grungy skater kid with chin-length hair and a chain wallet. The minute I saw him leaning against the cement wall that wrapped around the front of the school, I was lost. The best part? He was my friend's older brother.

Being a teenager was not easy for me. I don't think it is for anyone, but it's a different kind of hard when your body betrays you. Parts of it had started shifting and sprouting since fifth grade. I'd worn braces and glasses up until eighth grade, when my monster-mouth teeth had finally been tamed, and my mom had agreed to let me wear contacts. *Blue* contacts. My face gave away my age. Even with the permanent sneer, I looked young and dumb. My body was different. Older men whistled at me when I walked home from school, but I had absolutely no confidence in my physical appearance. Who would want me, right?

But somehow introductions were made, and by the third and last week of school, I'd started to skip the afternoon class to hang out with Joe.

I took a drag off his cigarette and passed it back to him. The first time I'd almost choked, but now I managed to appear to look like I knew what I was doing. We stood on the corner of Schuster and Virginia trying to hide from the sun and campus security. Both were equally bothersome.

"Are you going to class?" he asked, taking the cigarette from my fingers.

As his fingers brushed mine, I swear I felt little snaps of electricity like fresh clothes from the dryer.

I shrugged, "I don't know. I should—"

He interrupted and grinned. "But you're not gonna?"

I smiled. Silent. I'd already missed two classes because I'd slept in. A third would mean I'd wasted the first two weeks of my time for Geography II. I swallowed the smoky taste and gazed back up the street to the school.

I should go to class.

But as quickly as the thought came, it left when Joe pulled me closer to him by one of my belt loops. He draped his arm around my shoulders and a rush of heat flooded my cheeks as I looked up into his blue eyes. I'd never been this close to him. He smelled like incense and cigarettes. I licked my lips, but suddenly my mouth was as dry as the mountainside the school sat on.

"Come on, let's go smoke." His eyes met mine.

"Okay," I croaked out.

He flicked the butt onto the sidewalk and winked, "Let me go get the guys."

And as quickly as he'd pulled me against him, he moved away and started to walk back toward the school. I didn't have time to think about what guys he was talking about or why he'd pulled me against him so quickly and then just as quickly let me go because after a few steps he turned and called out, "Come on!"

I nodded and followed him up the hill. There we found the guys. Hank and Angelo. They were all a lot taller than me, thin with baggy pants, and scuffed skate shoes.

"We gonna smoke? Or what?" Joe asked.

Hank grinned, toothy, and nodded. Angelo stared at me without smiling and gave a single nod. He eyeballed me, up and down. "Who's this?"

I tugged down the t-shirt that showed an inch of skin above my baggy jeans.

Joe said, "She's cool. Don't worry."

This was my last chance to bail. Instead, I crossed the street with them and started to climb up and into the mountain. The guys talked about papers and getting a nickel from some dude named Felix. I had no idea what they were talking about. I eyed the copper point above us marking the end of the Rocky Mountains, then looked back at the school.

"Where are we going?" I asked, a little out of breath. If I had known we were going hiking, I would have passed.

They seemed to forget they were each about six inches taller than me, maybe more, and their single step was almost three of mine.

"The jungle," Joe replied.

I contemplated the sloped makeshift path and wondered what jungle he was talking about. Most of the cactus and creosote along the walk were a faded green or brown. Nothing that remotely looked like a vibrant jungle, but I nodded as if I knew what he meant.

"Here"—he held out his hand—"I'll help you."

My cheeks warmed again, but this time it wasn't from the hike. I placed my hand in his and prayed it wasn't clammy gross.

He helped me with the larger steps up that he took with little effort. Sweat started tickling my lower back. It was maybe a ten- to fifteen-minute walk, but parts of it were steep, and my feet couldn't tread where other, longer legs had already created makeshift steps. I was really regretting this decision. *What was I thinking?*

The sweat dampened the short hair along my neck. By the time we got to this stupid jungle, I was going to be a sweaty mess. They were sweating too, but I was a girl. Sweaty rules were different for girls. My mind was spiraling, but then I saw the last steep step up to what seemed like a small flat space. *Great! How am I going to get up there?*

Joe had let go of my hand because the last move was hard even for him. He reached up with both hands and pulled himself up. I paused, glanced down, then back up.

"You can do it," he said with a smile.

That sweet stupid smile.

I tried to do what he just did, hopped up, tried to pull myself up. Instead I slid down the side, not all the way, but my hands got full of orangey dirt, one leg straight behind me, the other bent against my body. A yoga master would have been proud of my involuntary pigeon pose.

Joe started to laugh. My stomach dropped all the way down that stupid mountain. *What the fuck? This wasn't funny.*

"Dude, fuckin' help her," Angelo said.

"Okay. Okay," Joe said. "My bad."

He took my hand. After a minute, I managed to pull myself up. My jeans, hung low on my hips, slid a little lower and were full of dirt. So were my suede Vans. I tried to dust my hands off on my butt, but I just grabbed more sand. When I looked up, I saw Hank and Angelo sitting on the edge of an old mattress someone must have somehow brought up here. That person had to be crazy. I couldn't imagine carrying a full-sized mattress all the way up this steep hill.

"Welcome to the Jungle," Joe said.

The other two snickered, but it was obvious this had to be the hundredth time he'd told the joke. He sat alone against a tree. There was no room next to him. I looked from him to the space next to Angelo, thinking he would get my drift, but he didn't move. I bit my lip and crouched down to sit next to Angelo. Hank was busy with a plastic sandwich bag in his lap.

That's when I realized what Joe had meant by "smoke." We didn't hike up here to smoke cigarettes. *Oh my god. What had I gotten myself into?*

If I had been silent before, now I was completely tongue-tied. Immediately, I pictured my mom and a K-9 officer in their blue Customs uniforms, standing on the stage at Lamar

Elementary, talking about drug abuse. Don't do drugs!! The red-lettered logo D.A.R.E. on the t-shirts they gave out as prizes flashed like a neon sign. Shit!

I turned to see Hank licking a white paper shut.

"Don't goob that shit, dude," Joe said looking at Hank.

I glanced from his face to Angelo's. "Goob?"

Angelo turned to me, his face close. "Spitty."

I had been so focused on Joe before that I hadn't noticed Angelo's accent.

"Where are you from?"

"Italy."

His dark eyes lingered on me. I tucked and untucked my hair behind my ears.

"Yeah, you didn't know? This dude's our very own Italian Stallion," Joe said, reaching for the joint Hank had lit.

I smelled the earthy scent and gulped. It went from Hank, to Joe, then Angelo, but instead of hitting it, he passed it to me.

"First the lady."

My eyes darted from his face to the smoking joint in his hand and back again. I glanced at Joe and Hank and all three stared at me. I didn't have a choice. Before I knew what to do, my body reacted with a mind of its own. I took the joint and held it as I had seen them hold it, pinched between thumb and index finger, and put my lips to it. I took a short inhale. *If I took a couple puffs, I would be okay, wouldn't I?*

The funky taste filled my mouth. Grassy. Then a burn spread to my lungs that I had never felt before, and I coughed. Hard. A coughing fit racked my body, and my eyes burned. The guys all laughed as I held the joint out to Angelo.

"Someone is going to be bla-zed," Joe said.

Hank giggled.

They passed the joint a couple more times, but I shook my head when it came to me. That was the worst feeling ever. If choking on a cigarette had been horrible, this was a thousand times worse. Hank smoked it down to the nubbiest of nubs and only stopped when he yelped and shook his hand. Then he giggled. Then the other two giggled. I looked from each of their faces and forced a giggle too. *What were we laughing at?*

They giggled a little longer.

"Dude, this weekend is going to be cra-zy. That chick, Teresa, she's having a thing."

Hank sat grinning and nodding. I wrapped my arms around my bent legs and rested my chin on my knees. Somehow, I thought this would be funner. *Wait, is funner a word?* I frowned.

"She has that place, right?"

"Yup."

From here, in the break of the trees, I could see the school. Kids walked in front and around the corners until they disappeared.

"Right on."

I turned to look at them again. Angelo, though, stared at me. His dark eyes met mine. We stared at each other for a minute until I got a weird feeling in my stomach. Dude made me feel like if I'd done something wrong. I turned away and let my black hair curtain my face from his. A few minutes later, Hank finally spoke.

"I better go, bro. My mom is coming for me."

I nodded. Ready to go. If this was what smoking was, I didn't like it. I didn't even feel anything.

We walked back down. I slid a couple of times, but by this time, I didn't care. I just had to make sure I dusted myself off like crazy before I got to Ita's. At the school, we parted ways. I'd hoped that Joe would hang around to talk to me, maybe even put his arm around me again, but he didn't. He just waved, put his hands in his pockets and walked toward Mesa Street. What a waste of an afternoon. *Why had I thought—ugh: he was just like everyone else.*

Before I walked home, I brushed at the dust that clung to my jeans and stomped on the sidewalk to get it off my shoes. My hands were grimy with a layer of sand that wouldn't shake off. When I turned onto our block, I saw the parking spaces were empty. *No one was home!* I did a little jump. Ita was usually home. *Where was she?* Wait, it didn't matter.

I ran the half block, skipped up the stairs, put my key in the door, turned, and went straight to the bedroom to get Drew, then to the bathroom. I set her down on the floor, turned the handles on the bathtub, and held my hand under the running water to check the temperature.

"Meow?"

I glanced over. Drew sniffed my shoes.

"I know, okay? You don't have to tell me," I mumbled to her.

The water ran brown from my dirt-coated hand. I rinsed it till the water ran clear, then undressed and stepped into the tub. I leaned against the back and let out the breath I didn't know I had been holding since I'd said yes to Joe. Drew curled into a ball, laid inside my jeans, and licked her paws.

Later, I sat watching MTV in my mom's room when Ita called me.

"Prieta! Teléfono!"

I grabbed the handset from her and the base with the other hand. I pulled the cord and made my way to her room so she wouldn't hear.

"Hello?"

"*Duuuddeee,*" my friend Mia's voice came through the phone.

"What? What?" I asked, my chest suddenly fluttering.

Ita's room was dim in the late afternoon light. I sat wide-eyed at the foot of her bed waiting to hear whatever had to be big news.

"You made an impression today."

"Whha—?"

"At the jungle! I can't believe you went there. You said you weren't gonna miss anymore." Her voice cackled on the other end.

I stared at my reflection in the dresser mirror and scrunched my face. That's what I *had* said.

"But, wait . . . what impression? Did Joe say something?"

"No, dude. No Joe. Fuck that guy." There was a pause, "*Angelo.* He asked me to ask you if he could call you. He's pretty *hot,*" she sang.

I peered at myself again. Eyes wide. *Angelo??* That guy? I flashed back to today, to his face as he stared at me. He seemed so serious. Wary of me even. Some intense stink eye. I thought he'd hated me or something. *That* guy wanted to call me?

"Well?" Mia asked on the other end.

I'd been quiet longer than I thought. I shrugged.

"I mean . . . I guess."

I slumped lower into the bed.

"Dude, come on. He's hot, and he likes you."

"Yeah, I guess you're right."

"I mean it's just a call. If he's dumb or something, just say you gotta go."

"Wait, you mean he's gonna call like right now?"

She giggled, "Mmmhhmmm. Why do you think I called? I already gave him your number."

"Dude!"

She laughed. Then I heard it. The buzz.

"Oh my god. It's the other line."

My eyes met in the mirror, wide.

"What? *Ohmygod! Ohmygod!* Answer that shit!"

"*What?!*" I whisper-shrieked.

"Dude! Yasmín! Answer!"

I nodded, "You better call me aft—"

I switched over to the other line. "Hello?" I whispered.

TWENTY-ONE

I WAS FIFTEEN when I tried to reconnect with my father. I had thought I might try again. And this time—I thought—it would be different. This time, he would be the parent he was supposed to be.

Angelo and I had been together for over a year. That first phone call had somehow morphed into a classic high school romance of the cheerleader and high school quarterback, except we weren't quite those people. Instead of sports and school spirit, we bonded over our general rebellion of—well—anyone who told us to do something we didn't want to, and our lack of fathers. His mother had moved him to the States from Italy around middle school, after his father had disappeared. Angelo would be a giant part of my life for the next five years. That would prove to be both a good and bad thing for me.

It was my sophomore year, and we were still in the thick of young love when Angelo found out my father lived in El Paso. He didn't understand why I didn't try to see him. It was lunchtime. We'd just smoked a bowl and sat leaning against a tree next to the dirty old mattress where we'd first met in the Jungle.

"You should see him." He nudged at me with his elbow.

I sat with my arms wrapped around my body inside of oversized overalls and stared into the twisted cluster of trees that really just seemed like oversized weeds. I wished we'd brought water.

"I—I don't think it's a good idea." I licked my dry lips. "I mean, you don't know what he was like after we got divorced."

He stayed quiet for a moment. "I would do it."

We both fell still. The dare he'd laid between us nestled into the sandy ground. My silence buried it though. When I didn't respond after a few moments, he tried again.

"I'm gonna be with you. This time you won't be alone."

"My mom was there all the other times. It didn't change anything."

"That was different." He sighed.

I gazed into his dark, bloodshot eyes, that so often looked guarded and found one of those rare moments when he didn't look like he was waiting for something bad to happen. At first, I didn't recognize the expression, but then I understood. There was that fucking hope again.

"Fine. Okay," I shrugged.

We were back on the Eastside now. After about a year, just as abruptly as we had packed to move in with Ita, we boxed everything up and moved back. So when I told my mom I was going to see my father, she simply nodded. Except her eyes said it all. She hovered and watched as Angelo and I drove away one early Saturday afternoon. I don't know why I know this, because I can't even remember the make of

Angelo's shitty old gray car, but I know we drove to my dad's house out on the edge of northeast El Paso on a Saturday.

When we walked in, I saw the small remodeled garage was almost exactly the same as when I had been there several years before. While my dad and I were about the same height, Angelo's tall, broad frame seemed too large for the room. In the cramped space, I pushed at my hair, tucked it behind my ear, only to push at it again.

I hadn't said more than a handful of words to my dad since we'd knocked on the door. I hadn't called. I just wanted to go and see what his face looked like, eyes wide and a little uneasy, when he saw me. This time I couldn't be left waiting.

My dad just smiled and pointed me in the direction of the couch while he went somewhere to grab a chair. When he left the room, I peered at Angelo with wide eyes, and he gave me a small smile. I took a breath and sat.

I gazed up at the wall behind him and saw a row of frozen smiling faces hung along the top edge where the ceiling and wall met. My dad had continued to hang my half-siblings' school photos. They wrapped onto another wall. In each, of course, they were a little bit older.

"Is that you?" Angelo pointed.

In the earlier photos, I saw my lone kindergarten face.

I nodded. I was eternally a six-year-old in this house.

My dad came back with a metal folding chair he placed at the corner where a desk and the couch met. They both hugged a wall. Angelo sat, folding his long legs under it as best he could. My dad went to the fridge.

"¿Quieren algo?" he asked.

I shook my head, "No. We're okay."

I heard the *pop* of a beer can. So even though I said we were fine, he held out a yellow and gold Coors can to Angelo and sat in the chair in front of the desk. Angelo stood, took the beer, tapped the top, popped, and sat back down in the small space between us.

"Bueno, mija. ¿Pues, cómo estás?" He glanced from my face to Angelo's with a grin.

My mom always said the best thing I ever got from him was my smile. As he looked at us, I could see the toothy similarity even with the dark beard that hid a bit of his top lip.

"I'm good, Dad."

Dad. The syllable felt foreign, leaving my mouth.

"¿Y tú mama? Does she know you're here?"

I cringed a bit when he spoke English. His accent was thick and choppy. Even though Ita had one, it was a whisper. His was a crass woman yelling down the street. I also heard the bite in his voice when he asked about my mom, but I ignored it. Kinda.

"Yeah. Of course." I shrugged. "Why wouldn't she?"

He paused mid-sip. It was his turn to shrug, "No, nomás preguntando."

I crossed my arms across my chest. Angelo glared at me. I let my arms fall and tried to smile, but we fell silent while they both sipped their beers. I realized that I hadn't thought about what I was going to say once we *got* here. I'd been so worried about coming that I'd never planned what would happen once I was with him. I glanced from Angelo to my dad and back. That's when I saw my dad grin again. He was practically beaming beneath that beard.

"How is everyone?" I finally asked.

My smile felt forced. My eyes floated around the small space and toward the door. I reached for my hair again but tried to still my hands in my lap. As he spoke, I wasn't really listening. I just took him in. The way he sat with the can of beer between his legs even though the desk, which he must use as a table, was in front of him. His black hair, hair like mine, was a little shaggy the way it fell over his forehead. As he spoke, he gestured with his broad, calloused hands.

I wondered if he still worked as a carpenter. As a small child, I'd gone to his shop a handful of times. The *taller* was always covered with sawdust from the kitchen cabinets and countertops they made. I swept it with a broom twice my size into neat little piles, even though the dust appeared again and again.

One time, I even made a friend, a small brown mouse who must have lived in the shop. My mom had to have been working. I don't know why I wasn't with Ita. They must have been fighting, but I spent the day there, moving around the midsized *taller* as the mouse scurried back and forth. Sometimes it came out, and I ran as it chased me. Other times, I played peek-a-boo with it as it hid under the spaces between tall lumber stacks. I wanted to pet its soft brown fur but knew I couldn't. We played almost the whole day. The last time it ran out, it started to scurry across the long stretch of dusty concrete floor. I began to chase it but stopped when I saw my dad holding a slim piece of angled wood. He stood with his coworkers. As he lifted his right arm, they laughed and pointed.

I screamed, but it was too late. My brown mouse was

dead, pierced by the wood. My mouth opened into a big, round silent O at my mouse's blood against the gray concrete. My dad and his workers high-fived each other until I burst into tears. He rushed to pick me up and tried to hug me, but I pushed away from him with my small hands. I cried and cried until my mom got there.

"Y bueno, eso es lo que ha estado pasando aca, mija."

Even though I'd been staring at him the whole time, I realized I hadn't really heard anything he'd said. He'd just finished telling me what was happening here, and I hadn't heard any of it. I looked at Angelo and back at my dad. Angelo made the slightest gesture with his eyes that I knew meant *say something,* but I didn't have anything to say. What do you say to a man you haven't seen in three years? His hands had sparked the memory of my mouse. Now it was all I could think about.

No one said anything, like we were all asleep. Then I saw it again: the grin on his face.

"¿Qué es lo que me querían preguntar?"

"What did we wanna—" my voice faded. "What?" I asked.

What did we want to ask him? Then it hit me. The look. The giant grin. The way he kept glancing at both of us. My cheeks flushed, and he grinned even more. I glanced at my hands and up at the door. A mix of emotions I'd never felt before swirled inside me, and I wanted to run. I needed to get out of there. I didn't belong here. I tucked my hair behind my ears.

"Nothing. I, we, just came to say hi." I stood, bumping my knee against the desk. "But now we have to go."

Angelo looked up at me, wide-eyed, Coors can still in

his hand.

The grin fell from my dad's face, "¿Tan pronto?"

I nodded quickly and moved toward Angelo. I tugged at his t-shirt sleeve.

"Yeah, it was just a quick hi. Just to saludar."

I took the half-full beer can from Angelo's hand, set it on the desk, and tugged at his sleeve again. *Why wasn't he moving?*

My dad looked back and forth from our faces again, but this time he wasn't grinning. His eyebrows were pinched, both centers curving up, just like mine when I'm confused. I turned toward the door again. I didn't know where to look. I didn't want to meet his eyes. The room felt smaller than before. If that was even possible. I pushed at the front door. Angelo finally stood. I felt his size behind me.

"Bueno, mija."

"We just wanted to start coming so Yasmín could see you more," Angelo tried to explain.

"Si, sí. Cuando quieran."

I didn't turn to look back at them. Their voices sounded slow, as I popped out onto the gravel driveway. Angelo said something else behind me, and my dad followed. I wasn't listening anymore.

"Okay, bye." I waved, turning and moving down the driveway backward.

I was already halfway to the sidewalk when Angelo shook my dad's hand.

In the car, Angelo said, "What the fuck just happened?"

"Can you drive? I wanna get out of here." I threw my head back against the seat.

"What the fuck? You were fucking rude."

I turned to glare at him as my dad's parent's house moved away.

"Don't you get it? He thought we were there to tell him we were getting married! That you were there to ask him for permission or some shit," I screeched. "I'm fucking fifteen. Did you see his face? Who's happy their fifteen-year-old daughter's getting married?"

Angelo frowned. "No—oh shit, I think you're right. That's why he was all smiling and shit?" He laughed.

I frowned. It wasn't fucking funny.

"Ohmygod. Ohmyfuckinggod." I slouched and covered my face in my hands. "Can you just take me home? This was the worst idea."

I stared out the window at the military uniform resale shops, Chinese buffet joints, and Mexican food places that lined Dyer Street. *Who was that man?*

"It wasn't that bad. He just doesn't know. You don't—"

"Stop. You just don't fucking get it, okay? Our dads aren't the same people. Just because you can't see yours doesn't mean I have to see mine. So, please, stop."

Angelo fell silent, but I saw the set of his mouth. The clenched jaw. I didn't care.

"I'm not doing that ever again."

I was seventeen when I tried to reconnect with my father again. And this time, I thought for sure—again—it would be different. This time, I was certain he would be the parent I hoped he could be.

Angelo and I were on a break from our relationship.

Well, technically we took, like, three different breaks that year. He had already graduated, and my plan to graduate with his class had changed. I was missing one AP English credit that I could have begged to test out of, but instead I stayed. I took two dance classes, an Intro to Spanish, AP English, and then left after lunch. It was the best senior year schedule anyone could have asked for. The fun I was having as dance team captain and a different set of friends from when we'd first met didn't mesh well with Angelo. I was having too much fun being a senior while he was trying his hand at community college.

So, though I cried and worried if we would get back together *this time*, a part of me was able to just be. When we'd first dated, I was in awe that he like *really* liked me. I'd always felt like someone's afterthought. Mom was always working, Angie was living her life, my dad was a ghost I kept chasing, and Ita, well, she was my Ita. She had to love me. Angelo was the first person who made me feel wanted. But, now that we were older, sometimes when I was with him, it was like I was holding my breath and I didn't even know it.

On this break, I don't know what sparked it, but I decided I wanted to reach out and try to get to know my dad and half-siblings. I was older and realized that relationships took work from both sides. I reasoned maybe I hadn't tried hard enough before. I'd given up too quickly. So this time, I called and asked him if we could hang out, and he agreed. I exhaled as I put the phone down.

Mom was in her room watching the Lifetime Network. Her favorite station. Since her promotion at the end of my sophomore year, she hadn't been on the bridge, yet her bedroom remained the same cluttered mess of laundry and paper from when I was younger. She even joked she'd finally gotten an eight-to-five gig to be with me when I just wanted to be with my friends. That was mostly true.

"Mom?"

"Que, mija?"

She was propped up by pillows. Remote in her right hand.

"So. I called my dad."

She turned down the volume, "¿Y qué te dijo?"

I shrugged and sat on the edge of the bed. "Nothing really. I mean, he seemed surprised, but why wouldn't he be, right?"

She nodded.

"I don't know." I smoothed the thin comforter. "I told him that I wanted to try to get to know him and the family, and he said yes. So"—I shrugged—"a ver."

She nodded again, "Well, baby girl, if that's what you want. Just be careful over there. Be on guard, okay?"

"On guard?"

"Yeah, quien sabe qué maldades piense esa gente de ti. They can say anything they want about me, but si te maltratan, they die."

I rolled my eyes. "*Mom,* it'll be fine. What are they gonna do to me?"

She raised her brows. "You never know. Just be careful."

That one phone call, at seventeen, resulted in two visits with my father. I had made a promise to myself that I would try. I would move through the awkward. Getting to know people was awkward, wasn't it? I had to give it time. We had to get to know each other.

The two memories of the visits are shrouded in a haze as if I'm not really there, as if I dreamt it, but I'm watching myself there at the same time. It's a feeling I can't shake, even now when I try to remember. I know I spent several hours with him, but I only have two short distinct memories. The images that tear through the cloud are flashes of shopping at a small market with my dad and having dinner with him, my half-sister, and her family.

The first memory took place at a small neighborhood market. I pushed a cart and followed him around while he bought groceries. He was the same squat barrel-shaped man. His broad back and thick arms seemed as if they should belong to a much bigger person.

When we got to the refrigerated section, he stopped for beer. Instead of grabbing a case, though, he started arranging them.

"You don't drink Coors anymore?" I asked.

The glass door was propped open with his body as he tugged at silver and blue Budweiser cases. When he turned to look at me, his face was just above the shopping cart.

"Pues no, mija. Ya que trabajo con Budweiser, ya no tomo eso."

I nodded and stayed quiet. I didn't understand what he was doing right now. I eyed the front of the store. The cashier's eyes were starting to linger in our direction. I shifted my feet and turned back.

"Um, what are you doing?"

"Es que no estaban bien," he pointed, "las cajas deben de estar así, but the person here, pues, no lo hicieron bien."

He grinned big at me like the day he'd grinned when Angelo and I were at his house. I studied the boxes he was rearranging. They did look neater, but why was he fixing the beer in a random store when he wasn't working? I peeked back at the store cashier who was now without batting an eye staring at us. I gave him a small smile and turned back as my dad explained more to me about how the boxes of beer should be arranged. I nodded, but an uncomfortable feeling crept from my stomach up into the back of my neck.

I smoothed the back of my shortly cropped hair.

After this break with Angelo, I'd visited my sister's friend with a picture of Sharon Stone sporting a short pixie. Since Angelo and I first met, my hair had grown out past my chin, and down to my shoulders in a shaggy Aniston. Each time I wanted to go shorter, Angelo told me how much he liked it, how pretty it was. I hated it, but left it. This breakup, I said fuck it, and cut it how I wanted.

But at this moment, I couldn't hide behind what wasn't there. I just gave a little smile. My cheeks were flushed from the cashier's stares. My dad kept moving boxes and talking, telling me more about Budweiser than I'd ever wanted to know.

Back home, I hadn't even put my keys down when my mom called out from her bedroom.

"How did it go, baby girl?"

I paused and walked down the hall toward her doorway. I leaned against the wood frame.

"It was . . . okay."

"What happened?"

"Nothing. Really. It was just—weird, you know? But everything is fine—"

Mom sat up, "Are you sure? You don't sound fine. ¿Te maltrataron?"

"No, no, Mom." I held my hand up. "No one was rude or mean. I swear. No one 'maltratar' me."

Her body relaxed slightly, but she didn't sit back as she had been before. I didn't want to talk about it, but I knew she wasn't going to let it go either. I moved to sit at the edge of her bed and told her about the day. When I got to the part at the store, I wouldn't look up to meet her eyes. I traced the stitching on her salmon-colored floral comforter.

"What's wrong, baby girl?" she asked quietly.

"I don't know. I just feel"—my voice cracked—"sad and weird about the whole thing, like even though I'm trying, we don't fit. We're too different." Tears slid down my cheeks. "He looked so happy at the store fixing that stupid beer, and all I wanted to do was hide. The cashier at the tienda kept staring at us, and I know I shouldn't care, but I did." I paused. "He's always going to be the man that's proud his fifteen-year-old is getting married. I think that's sad. He should want more."

Mom was silent as I cried. I heard her fumble with something on her nightstand. She pushed some tissue toward me.

I grabbed. "I feel like such a jerk."

"Ay, mija. Have I ever told you what your dad said once when you were little, and you asked how we met?"

I wiped at my face and shook my head.

"He said, 'I looked up at the sky, and shot for a star, and I got lucky.' Tu papá es un hombre muy simple."

Even after this initial visit and all the uncomfortable feelings, I gave it another try. I had to see this through. This time, I was going to my half-sister's house for lunch. She lived within blocks of where my dad lived. In fact, many of her—I guess mine too—tias and tios lived in the same neighborhood within walking distance from each other. I pulled up to her house and quickly found out I was thirty minutes earlier than I should have been. My dad wasn't there yet. Her children were there, but I don't remember a thing about them.

What I do remember was being in the backyard with her and handing her wet clothes to hang on the clothesline. I stood by the basket, and she asked about Angie. She told me little tidbits of when they were kids, and I felt a pang of jealousy. I had always been so much younger than Angie, I never felt the camaraderie that she was speaking about since they were closer in age. I wanted to hear more and then didn't. Now that Angie lived in Dallas, we talked even less. Outside of Angie, I don't know what we talked about. I wished I could dig it up and polish it until the memory was clear, but things don't work that way. Instead I have murky images with only one unclouded spot.

She made beef flautas. Several of us sat around a round table.

"Yasmín, ¿quieres ensalada?" she asked.

I nodded, "Yes. Thank you."

Even though I had offered to help, she'd shooed me out

of the kitchen. When a plate was handed to me, I saw four long beef flautas and chopped iceberg lettuce with sliced tomatoes, just like at Mexican restaurants, but not really a salad. I usually never ate this and thought of it as more of a garnish.

When everyone sat to eat, guacamole, crema, and salsa passed around, we were ready to dig in. Then someone called out, "La sal!"

I didn't want to be rude, so I paused mid-air with the flauta pinched between my fingers. Salt? Why did we need salt?

Then just as items were passed around the table before, a saltshaker made the rounds. When it got to me, I examined my plate and passed to my left. They had all added salt except me. I looked down at my plate.

My dad asked, "¿No le vas a poner salecita a la ensalada?"

"What? Er, um, no. I'm fine."

Salecita on lettuce? Why did lettuce need salt? Or the rest of the plate when they hadn't even tasted it? When my dad had suggested a meal at Geno's, I had looked forward to it. Food made things easier, conversation, stories, but now, I sat with my hands in my lap waiting for everyone to start eating. It was clear. They were a family, and I was just visiting.

When I got home, this is the moment that stood out to me. I told my mom about it, just as I had the last time, and it ended in a similar way. Instead of being embarrassed and ashamed of my embarrassment, this time the tears came from feeling so out of place even with a room of smiling people. It seemed that no matter how hard I tried, these people I was trying to make family were just strangers.

The third time I was supposed to hang out with my dad, something happened. I forgot we'd made plans.

I was parked outside a friend's house. She'd just gotten in the car. I turned the volume knob down as Everclear mumbled in the background.

"Mija, ¿estás en el camino?" His voice crackled through the phone.

I looked at my friend in the passenger seat, wide-eyed.

"On my way—no, Dad. I forgot to call you. I can't make it today."

She mouthed, "What?' but I just shook my head.

"Oh, bueno, mija. Te estaba esperando aquí, pero—" His voice trailed off.

I searched the car as if to find something, but I didn't know what. I glanced up at her house. I could go over there now, couldn't I? I looked at my friend's face. But then I would be letting my friends down. We'd already made plans.

"I'm sorry, Dad. I can call you this week, no? Or you can call me to tell me when you're off?"

I imagined him nodding as he said, "Si, mija."

That day, I went to a friend's house party. The early evening, I was a bit quiet trying to understand what had just happened. I swallowed the malty Bud Light and wrinkled my nose at the flavor. *How could I forget?*

Later, after a couple more beers that went down a bit smoother, I thought about the times he'd stood me up. I wondered what it had felt like for him. I also wondered if somewhere in the back of my mind, I had *wanted* to forget.

Just as I was pondering this, someone called out "Shots!" and a group of us all scurried to the kitchen.

I didn't call my dad that week. He never called either.

The last time I saw my father, I was nineteen. I showed up at his house on a Sunday night. I didn't want to try again. It wouldn't be different. He was never going to be the parent I'd hoped he'd be. Now, I just wanted to know why.

Chuck and I had been dating for a few months. We had both been through a rough break up. He'd lived with his girl when she'd suddenly moved out. I found out that Angelo had gotten another girl pregnant on the last break. He'd tried to hide it from me, but I still found out. Even though I felt relieved to have an out from our yo-yo relationship, the hurt and betrayal ran deep. I barely went to my classes at UT El Paso and spent more time dancing and partying my sorrows away than studying. Somehow, I danced my way to Chuck. He was a quirky guy who made me laugh. I needed to laugh. We both did.

After a night out, we ended up at an after-party where suddenly the conversation took a turn to everyone sharing stories of their amazing fathers. Chuck and I stared at each other. We were the only two in the cigarette-smoke-and-booze-bottle-cluttered room who didn't have that kind of story to share. He shrugged it off. I took in all their smiling faces and heartwarming stories. Each time I took a sip of beer, a knot in my throat grew bigger and bigger.

I tried to shake off the night. *Who talks about their fucking dads at an after-party?* I took a hot shower and brushed my teeth. *Fuck their dads.* I placed my contacts in their blue plastic container and put on my glasses. *Fuck them.* Once in my room, I turned on the TV and stared aimlessly at Madonna dancing in a cowboy hat on MTV. *Fucking fuckers.*

Drew, still small for her age, cuddled against my side. I gazed into her little face and tried to will it away, but the knot in my throat flamed. I blinked rapidly, but no matter how fast I blinked, Madonna blurred. I tried to swallow it back, but it escaped. The fortress I'd slowly been building around myself was closing in. I couldn't breathe. I was drowning. My chest heaved from the force. I was afraid my mom would wake up, so I pushed my face into a pillow. Part of me wished she would come, and the other part was horrified about what was happening to me. I didn't want any witnesses. All the things I'd been holding in—Angelo, failing my classes, my dad—all of it just poured out of me.

I don't know how long I cried, but when I woke in the morning, my head ached, and my eyes were two little slits hidden beneath tight inflated eyelids. Drew lay at my feet licking her paws. When my mom saw me, I had to explain what had happened. It sounded so stupid telling her I'd cried the better part of the night because some people talked about their dads at a party, but it was the truth. She hugged me, and I cried again. I spent the day in my room.

Near dusk, I found myself pacing. I scratched at my short hair. I took another shower. I got dressed.

Then, I called out, "Mom, I'm going to put gas in your truck."

Silence.

"Okay, mija."

It was early fall in El Paso, but I still walked out the door in a pair of jeans, t-shirt, and flip-flops. I put on my mom's aviators in the truck. It was less for the light and more for the swollen eyelids. I didn't know what I was doing, but I needed to get out of the house. I turned onto a main street, Montana, and drove west toward the mountains and orangey setting sun. The desert Ft. Bliss sand to my right looked ginger in the light. I pushed the oversized sunglasses up my nose and pulled into a random Chevron gas station I'd never been to before.

At the pump, I peeked at my phone.

"Hey girlie, wanna chill?"

Chuck. No. I did not want to chill. I stuck it in my back pocket without responding. I heard the *click* from the gas pump, put the handle back where it went, pushed at the sunglasses, and jumped back into my mom's lifted gray Toyota. In the parking lot, I sat with my blinker clicking to the left to go home, but when I saw an opening in traffic, I put the truck into first gear and turned right. I headed west, then northeast.

When I got to my dad's house, the sky was violet. I parked across the street, hopped down from the truck and walked to the chain-link fence that surrounded the house. I lifted the latch and marched toward the front door and knocked.

I didn't know if he still lived in the back house or whether he was there. The porch light flicked on and Mami Paola, my grandmother, opened the door.

"¿Diga?" she peered out through a slit in the main door and the screen of the outside one.

"Sí, ¿está Chuy?"

I couldn't make her face out well. She took a moment to answer.

"¿Quién lo busca?"

I swallowed. "Su hija."

She paused, didn't say anything, and gave one short nod before she closed the door. Why had I come here? *What kind of fucking grandma was she?* I wasn't even invited into the house. I started back down the walkway, unlatched the chain link, and stepped out onto the sidewalk. I moved toward the truck but froze. I'd already come this far. I walked toward the end of the driveway where he would see me.

I stood waiting, hands hanging by my sides, when I saw a familiar figure move down the driveway. He wasn't smiling this time, but he searched my face.

"¿Está todo bien?"

I nodded. "Yeah. Everything is fine."

Then I just stared at him. He peered up and down the street, at the truck, and then me.

"¿Entonces qué pasó, mija?"

Standing there, I felt an odd calmness I had never felt before when I'd visited him. For once, I didn't have to worry about what he thought of me—if I looked nice, if I was doing well, no *better*, than my half-siblings. I didn't have anything to prove. He missed his chance to be my dad. My hair stuck out at different angles, my eyes were still swollen, and the stale taste of tequila and cigarettes still lined my mouth, no matter how much I'd brushed.

"I want to know why, after the divorce, you never came to see me. You just"—I swung my arm into the air—

"disappeared."

"¿Qué?" He stepped back.

I shifted forward. "You just left. You stopped seeing me. You left me waiting. You just," I swallowed, "stopped being my dad. Like I didn't matter."

He stayed quiet for a moment. I stared at him, waiting. I wanted to hear what I'd done to make him disappear like that. Wanted to know why. Why I was never good enough for him to want me in his life.

"No, bueno, mija, tu mamá—"

"No," I interrupted.

"What?" He frowned.

"No. You don't get to do that. You can't blame my mom. I know. I know all the things she did for me while you weren't there. You don't get to use her."

The calmness that I'd arrived with disappeared with the flick of the streetlights coming on. My voice shook now. It was loud on that quiet block. I was glad my face was shadowed by the early night. All those years of talking about my feelings with a counselor had cooled my rage, but standing here, it ran hotter than I'd ever felt before. I hooked my thumbs on my back pockets so he couldn't see my hands shaking, to keep me from shoving him back into the fence.

"Pero, mija. We saw each other. But then you got older, and you wanted to go with your friends . . . "

"That was one time," I held a shaky finger up between us, "one time I forgot."

He shifted back again. Now it was my fault. My eyes fell from his face. I felt the burn again from last night, but I wouldn't cry in front of him. This wasn't what I was looking for. I kept coming back, but I didn't know what I wanted, and each time, I left more and more disappointed. Empty. I stared at the way the light glittered on the mica in the sidewalk, then at the white house behind him, and finally at him. He was still talking, saying things, but none of them were right. He babbled.

"Okay. I'm leaving now," I interrupted.

He jumped at my voice, then stood frozen as I crossed the street toward the truck. When I opened the door, he called out, "Be careful." I froze, my back toward him for a second, then pulled myself up.

I got two blocks down when I had to pull over. Fresh tears ran down my hot face. The truck idled. I didn't know where to go or what to do. I ran my hand along the seat until I found my phone.

"Hello?"

"Aaa-nge." I hiccupped.

"Yasmín. What's wrong?"

I heard the concern flood her voice, but I couldn't breathe enough to talk.

"I-I cc-ame to see my Dd-ad," I heaved, "a-and hhe tried to bb-blame everything on mmmom, on meee."

"Are you driving? Pull over."

TWENTY-TWO

SOMETHING HAPPENED TO me. The bits and pieces of glue that had kept me together after Angelo, after visiting my dad, they just dissolved. I hung out with Chuck more. We partied more. I failed out of school and was put on academic suspension. My mom had one rule for me: "Do well in college, and you don't have to work."

She only asked one thing, and I fucked it up. So—I got a job. Other than a brief summer stint at a Tropical Sno, a snow cone place where I read my books most of the day inside the small air-conditioned booth, I'd never had a real job. I'd always earned money and privileges by doing well in school. Now I was stuck. I really don't know how I ended up working at the El Paso International Airport as a server/bartender, but I did.

The first few weeks, I hated every minute of it. I'd never worn a uniform before. When I studied myself in the polo shirt and baseball hat, I felt like Niño Yasmín. Ita had started to call me that after I'd cut my hair into a pixie. I didn't want her to know, but she had planted a seed, so I made sure to accentuate my already large brown eyes with eyeliner and mascara. I was tall by El Paso standards, a whopping five feet, five inches, but that was also the height of a lot of the guys I worked with, so it was one of the rare times when I was glad for the curve in my hips and boobs—or else I really would have looked like a scrawny boy.

I took food orders most of the time. The Tex-Mex menu was filled with pickled jalapeños and sour cream toppings that travelers thought were Mexican, but it made me queasy. Food service was gross. Sometimes I was lucky, and I got to cover one of the bars. I liked bar service better. It made me feel like Ita.

This was my routine: I got up, got dressed, went to work, went home, showered, and went out—sometimes with Chuck, sometimes with friends, but I went out more than I stayed home. The days morphed into one with everyone in the airport going somewhere, pulling rolly bags, while I stood still—either behind or in front of a bar.

It was March, three months in, when I realized something had to change.

Quick.

Chuck and I sat at a bar off the main strip in Juárez. It was a weekday, so we were two of only a handful of people there. One of the benefits of living on the border was being able to take a quick five-minute walk so I could drink when I was only eighteen. It was completely normal to cross over the concrete arc and find a bunch of teens with fake IDs barhopping the night away along Avenida Juárez. The street was like two open arms filled with bright neon lights and loud music beckoning us in with the promise of cheap drinks. Lots of places were open until six a.m., so the party only stopped when the money ran out. It was easy to get lost.

We sat in the dark bar with beer signs and TVs sprinkled around the room.

"Dos shots de tequila," I ordered.

The bartender nodded.

"Damn, woman, you wanna get all crazy on a Tuesday?" Chuck asked.

I shrugged and gave a half-hearted laugh. We swallowed the warm fiery liquid. I nursed the rest of my Dos Equis. Chuck had a point. *What was I doing?* I stared up at the TV screen playing Outkast's "So Fresh and So Clean." Andre 3000 and Big Boi danced with their little swing. They seemed like they were having a great time, and that's all I wanted. I wanted to have a good time, but more and more, little hints that this wasn't really a great time kept slipping in.

I surveyed the half-empty bar, then studied Chuck. He and I were just supposed to have been something light and fun, but now we were together more and more. I was jumping from one boat to another. I didn't even know what Chuck wanted to do with his life. I grabbed the green bottle by its neck and tilted it back. *I didn't even know what I wanted to do with my life!* Was sitting in a dingy bar on a weekday part of it?

I don't know what happened that night, but I decided to move to Dallas and Chuck headed for San Francisco. Maybe it was the bar, maybe the warm shots. Or maybe it was that, even in this dim light, we couldn't hide anymore from the truth about our lives.

It helped that Angie and I talked more after I'd called her when I left my dad's. I think that moment was the start of a very, very slow shrinking of our ten-year gap. Before then, she did Angie, and I—well, unless I was in trouble—did Yasmín. She'd moved to Dallas with her boyfriend Gabe five years before, but she was lonely. I don't remember exactly how the conversation went, but a week after my twentieth birthday, I found myself sitting in an empty bedroom on the second floor of her home in one of the many suburbs of Dallas.

Angie had come to El Paso to drive me home with her. I ate Hot Cheetos while Drew meowed, and Angie drove. The first thing I did when we got there was cry. The image of my mom waving from outside our house, just as my Ita had done when I was a kid, stuck in my head. I was nine hours away from home. Drew, who my mom insisted I take even when Angie hesitated, wouldn't come out from under the bed. I coaxed and coaxed, even though—really—I just wanted to crawl under there with her.

Life with Angie was very different. Mom often joked that I had two moms since Angie acted more like a mom than my sister. In this case, it was what I needed. At twenty, I now had a curfew. I had to work *and* go to school at the same time—and if I failed, I had to move out. I didn't have to pay rent, but I did have to buy groceries and help around the house. I didn't have a choice except to make it work.

I *needed* this if I was going to do better.

TWENTY-THREE

LIFE IN DALLAS—WELL, that was very different too. I got a job almost instantly at a place called Garden Ridge. It was like a Costco-sized Hobby Lobby. Eventually it became At Home. It was not my ideal job, mostly because I stood in the same five-foot square for extended periods, but like my mom says, "Beggars can't be choosers."

I worked as a cashier while furiously searching for a better job. Since I'd arrived mid-semester and my grades were crap, I had to wait until summer to go to a local community college to get my GPA up. So, as I swiped lily-scented candles and spring tablecloths, I applied at places in the nearby Lewisville Mall. Angie suggested retail since I didn't like food service, so I went with it.

We lived in the north suburbs of a city near Denton. I quickly learned that only new transplants and tourists referred to the entire Metroplex as Dallas. I also rapidly discovered no one knew where El Paso was or they thought it was in Mexico. I learned to make a map of the state with my hand. Pinky and ring finger bent, middle and index extended, and thumb flush against the palm. I pointed to the tip of my thumb.

"This is where El Paso is. It's not in Mexico," I said

countless times.

When I was younger, there were a few times when lighter-skinned Mexican kids had picked on me for being browner, but at home there was always some other brown kid next to me so I never felt out of place. Here, though, I had never been so aware of my brown skin as I was those first few weeks. It felt like I had an angry red pimple on my face, except it was my entire body. At lunch in the small break room, a male employee asked, "Where'd you learn to speak English so good?"

My mouth fell open. I glanced at the tuna sandwich in my hand and back up at his ruddy white face.

"El Paso. I'm from El Paso. El Paso is in Texas. West Texas."

I thought if I said El Paso and Texas enough times, it would sink in because even as I said it, his blond eyebrows wrinkled, and his mouth twisted up, unconvinced.

This was the start of *many many many* assumptions about my ethnicity and nationality. Everywhere I went, people asked where I was from? What part of Mexico? Why did I speak English so well? What was I? A common assumption was that I was Indian or Pakistani. A Pakistani woman yelled at me once when I told her I was Mexican American. "You Pakistani!" she grunted as she took her shopping bags. It seemed that Dallas—sorry, the metroplex—didn't have a lot of Latinas like me. At least, I never really found any, and I got used to it.

It was here that I learned to walk an interesting tightrope that many brown people face. I was always going to be brown to white people. Even later, when I made friends, they naively asked me to talk to servers at Mexican restaurants. Sometimes when I went to some of the authentic taquerias in areas like Oak Cliff, areas that had a heavy Latino population, *they* eyed me funny too. Their eyes held judgment as I stumbled over my words. There I was *pocha,* a term used to describe brown people like me who aren't fluent in Spanish. I have a gringa, North American, accent.

¿Pero cómo?

El Paso was easy. I understood all the Spanish because of Ita, my mom, the city. I easily slipped in and out of phrases, but a whole conversation? Nope. Never. It was easier just to speak English since I had to work at my Spanish. But in Dallas, my Spanish was reserved for *unos tacos de asada* or *más salsa por favor.* And, the longer I lived there, the more and more my Spanish faded.

But I'm jumping ahead.

I got a job at Victoria's Secret a short time after working at Garden Ridge. The fruity body splash smell, brightly colored lingerie, and pink everything were definitely more fun to be around. A lot of the girls at work were also in college at Brookhaven Community College, where I was enrolling, University of North Texas, or Texas Women's University. I was there to go to school so even though I made friends—and I did go out some—I remained focused.

After getting my grades up at Brookhaven, I was accepted to North Texas. Ange and Gabe took me to Chili's to celebrate. My four years at UNT are a blur, honestly. Snippets of bickering with Angie about who ate whose leftovers, some side-eyes for getting home past curfew, learning to cook, and going to Chili's down the street when something I made was not at all good. (Tip: There is such a thing as putting too much citrus on salmon.)

The first couple years, I was lonely. Even though I met people, it wasn't the same as at home. I called Ita and Mom often, but after we got off the phone, I felt lonelier. Back home, I had friends I'd grown up with, who really knew me, and I wasn't finding that here. Sometimes the story is that kids go away to college and fail, but I was the opposite. I had to move away to be successful, because at home there was always a party to go to or a friend to have fun with. Mom says I'm like Ita, we never wanted the party to end.

Now I sat in large classrooms with an ocean of faces. A lot of the time I felt as if I were an island of one. Angie was my anchor. I also understood why she struggled. The Metroplex was not warm and quick with a smile or a conversation like El Paso. *Era más difícil encontrar la buena gente.* The good people were hidden away from all the twisting and turning highways eternally under construction, parking lot traffic jams, and blond women with their faux *bless your heart* veneers.

Four years later when I graduated—on the Dean's List—with a degree in psychology, Mom and Ita came to my graduation. Their faces were bright with smiles and rosy cheeks.

On the way to the auditorium, Angie said, "For a while, I wasn't sure if you were gonna get here."

I could feel my smile dim. I stared down at my cap and gown and the sheen didn't seem as bright either.

"Yo, sí, mija." Mom squeezed my arm. "You just had to do things in your own time."

I nodded. They were both right. They gave me the balance I needed as I moved toward the next thing. Whatever that was.

TWENTY-FOUR

I HAD A plan when I started at UNT: Go to school. Get good grades. Take the GRE. Apply for clinical psychology programs. Get accepted. Move. Be successful.

Everything I had done since I'd moved in with Angie had worked toward that goal. I felt as if I had to make up for wasted time. My first round of college had gone poorly. I had to do better. My senior year, I'd volunteered for psychology studies to help build my skinny resume. I also volunteered as a student assistant to psychology grad students.

Still, twice a week, a grad student let me into a large closet where I attempted to organize files that ten other student assistants had already tried to tackle. The sheer mass of the variously colored file-folder stacks had overwhelmed them, and I could tell they'd run away. Hell, I wanted to run away, too, but I couldn't. I needed letters of recommendation for grad school, so I sorted dusty files and found a few brown bug carcasses along the way. After a few weeks, the grad students either had pity on me or I'd passed the hazing. I was taken out of the closet and brought into the office with them and assigned data-entry tasks.

It was there, one day shortly before graduation that

things were turned upside down. I sat at a desk entering numbers into an Excel sheet. One male grad student sat at a desk across from me. The only sounds were the clicks of our fingers across keys and the light buzz of some local radio station.

"Why do you want to go to grad school?" he asked.

I glanced up from the screen. I wasn't even sure he was talking to me. But I scanned the musty office cluttered with stacks of paper and full of filing cabinets and saw we were indeed the only ones there. The other grad student, a girl, had walked out without me noticing.

"Because I have to," I said, blinking at the spreadsheet on my computer screen.

"Who said?"

I shrugged and turned back to the screen. He stared at me for a moment then went back to his own screen. I wouldn't look at him. I just kept typing. But with each keystroke, his question clicked in my mind. *Why* did I want to go to grad school?

The long walk across the green campus was a haze. I didn't understand why his question had shook me so much, but when I stopped to think, I heard my voice, "Because I have to." *What kind of answer was that?* I hadn't said that because he'd caught me off guard. I'd said that because I didn't have a better response. The laughter and noise from other students on campus was muted as I mulled over it. I sat in my car staring at squirrels run up and down trees for a few minutes before even putting the key in the ignition.

The grad student, whose name I don't remember, shattered my life plan. Because, again, I *had* a plan when I started at UNT: Do well. Graduate. Take the GRE. Apply to clinical psychology programs. Thank Angie and Gabe profusely. Move to the best school that accepted me.

But only four of those things happened.

I had already taken the GRE and was waiting on the scores to see which clinical psych programs I would apply to. I was researching schools and the cost of living. But suddenly I was left asking myself why I was going down this path. *Who had said I should?*

I pulled into the mall parking lot. I had to go to work, but instead I sat in my car, crying. I called Mom and told her the story. She listened without interrupting.

"Mom, if I don't go to grad school right away, will you be disappointed in me?" My voice shook with tears.

She didn't answer. I tried to imagine her face. I'd already disappointed her before. I didn't want to do that again.

"Ay, mija. Of course not."

I got off the phone with her and gazed at the beige and tan exterior front of the mall. I couldn't work at the Victoria's Secret at Vista Ridge Mall forever. *What was I going to do now?*

TWENTY-FIVE

I WAS TWENTY-FIVE. It was a year after graduation, and I was living on my own. I'd applied at Neiman Marcus to work in Visual Merchandising. I'd worked the last year at Victoria's Secret doing windows and working on displays and found that I really enjoyed it, so I thought I'd give it a try. But on my application, Neiman's saw my lingerie experience, so to the sales floor I went. After several months, a bra vendor told me, "You should go work at Nordstrom, girl. It's busier, you'll make more money. Here." She wrote something on a piece of paper and held it out to me. "Go to Nordstrom. Ask for Vanessa Bahl."

And that's how I stumbled into the next five years of my life.

Now, I didn't know who this Vanessa Bahl was, but I thought, *What the hell.* So, I went to the Galleria Dallas Mall and had her paged from the Customer Service desk. When she came up from the basement offices, I introduced myself. She walked the lingerie sales floor with me, asked questions about vendors at Neiman's, and then told me to fill out the application. It seemed more of a formality because she was smiling from ear to ear. When I started a few weeks later, I learned that Vanessa Bahl was the regional manager for the southern U.S. Usually, she was traveling throughout the lower half of the country visiting various lingerie sales floors in all the stores sprinkled around the country. What seemed ballsy and brave had just been dumb luck.

Later, when I told my hiring story, which was a common thing to retell at the company, people were in awe.

"So—you just paged the Regional Manager of Lingerie?"

I always nodded and faked a know-it-all smile.

In my infrequent calls to my Ita, I tried to explain to her what I did.

"Sí, Ita. I'm working at Nordstrom. Es como Dillard's but fancier. Everything is more expensive."

I could hear the novelas in the background.

"¿Más caro?"

"Sí, Ita. But I get commission plus my salary as assistant manager, so it's good for me. I work at a new store. Se llama NorthPark. A mall where all the ricachones go to shop."

"Ah, Prieta. Está bien. Bueno, ya la dejo antes que le salga caro el bill del teléfono."

I smiled. Ita didn't understand cell phones didn't have long distance.

"Okay, Ita. I'm going to send you some fajas. The ones you like, okay? You liked the last ones I sent you, right?"

"Sí, Prieta. Sí."

After just a year at NorthPark Mall as an assistant manager, I was promoted to full manager of lingerie at the North

East Mall store in Hurst, Texas, about twenty-seven miles outside of Dallas. Even though the mall was tiny and the Nordstrom a small store compared to either the Galleria or NorthPark, I was excited to have my very own sales floor. I wanted to be a buyer now, and this was the next step toward that goal. I wanted to travel and go to trunk shows and pick the things the company would sell next season in the stores. All the brands and bags and sunglasses and shoes and, and, and, seduced me. Why was Prada so sexy?

When I first saw Jeffrey from across the sales floor, I fell in love. He was the tallest man I had ever seen. He was six feet, six inches with dark brown hair and green eyes. Where had he been all my life? Then I saw he was the "cool kid" of the men's department. Think every movie slow-motion shot of a handsome guy flipping hair out of his face. We all know the type. Bigger than life and knows it. I flashed back to any uncool moment in a teen movie where the new girl is trying to find where to sit and can't. *Then* I saw he was gay. I hated him and loved him more at the same time.

We became fast friends. Of course. We lived in fear of the store manager, Sheila, who made us work a ridiculous number of hours, but we survived together. (Is there a girl or woman named Sheila who is not "a mean girl"? If there is a nice Sheila out there, I want her to please prove me wrong.)

I often left for work when the sun was just rising and left work when it was already dark because anything less, even though small stores were far less busy, was not acceptable for Sheila. Her office was right by the employee entrance, and if any manager tried to leave at the end of their eight-hour shift, she called us out. She asked about our days's numbers, what we were doing to beat last year's, how we were we driving business—until we were shamed into walking back to our empty sales floor. Jeffrey and I often lamented Sheila and the long hours over our favorite lunch—chips and guacamole. We'd both worked at NorthPark, and North East paled in comparison.

After a year at Hurst, I was back at NorthPark Mall as the lingerie manager for the biggest-grossing sales floor in the Dallas Metroplex. I was ecstatic at first. But it lost its shine after about a year.

During my lunch breaks, I often ventured to the food court alone when Jeffrey and my other friends were too busy. (Shortly after I was promoted, Jeffrey made his way back to NorthPark too as manager of The Rail—aka the hip dude clothes department). I'd eat, and then I would pull out my dog-eared journal and write. Mostly I just journaled about my day. I wrote about how I felt. But many times, I wrote down the conversations I heard around me. People were willing to talk about some pretty personal topics in a food court. I faded into the background of the food court buzz and wrote scenes. Often the scenes didn't go anywhere, but it got me thinking. Did I really want to be a buyer?

A good friend had recently quit the company after having a regional manager position and traveling all over the place. The job had seemed so glamorous, but this is what she told me after she quit—"Yasmín, I could die, and no one would know I was gone. My parents, who are in Chicago, would be the only ones who would know I was missing. And even then, it would take them a few days because I'm always traveling, and no one knows where I'm supposed to be."

I went home alone to my townhome that day, and cuddled Drew while I watched TV. I scanned the place, filled with things, but it felt so empty. Her words echoed in my head. I needed something; I just didn't know what.

A few weeks later, I made a list. It was something like this.

Writing	Psychology
Happy	Learn
Read	Career
Learn	Financially stable
	Help people

Even though one list was longer than the other, one word stood out to me more than the others. Happy. Drew crawled into my lap.

"What do you think, Drew B.?"

She looked up and meowed. I had my answer. I got online. I researched. I gazed around my townhome again. Then I registered for some English classes at UNT. I didn't have enough English credits to apply for a graduate program in English/creative writing. When I asked my store manager if I could leave a little early on Wednesdays so I could make it to class on time, she assured me it was fine, but I noticed she smiled a smile that didn't quite reach her eyes.

When I think back on this moment, I realize it was the beginning of the end. If I could go back in time, to make things easier, I should have been smarter about everything, kept my fucking mouth shut.

Maybe my store manager knew before I did. Maybe skipping happy hour and going to school was a signal to the herd. Either way, this is the moment where things started to change for me.

So Ita didn't cause everything, but her death was the biggest fucking wake-up call of my life.

Era la gota que llenó el vaso.

The drop that filled the glass.

Jeffrey was the only man in my life for the longest time. Sure, I dated. I had sex. I moved on to the next guy, but Jeffrey was my companion. Often when we were together, people thought we were a couple. I couldn't help but grin when this happened. We laughed. He'd been with his partner Michael for longer than most straight couples. They bickered like it too. But Jeffrey was my heart. Jeffrey kept me sane. Jeffrey was one of the friends who was with me as I spiraled after my Ita's death.

TWENTY-SIX

There were signs that things were not going well for me even before Ita died. I can look back now and see them as clear as day. But I think when you're in the thick of whatever life has thrown at you, you make excuses, you find a way to deal. At least that's what I did. I missed all the signs, even though they were as clear as the painful headaches and queasy stomachs I suffered through.

"Gloria's on Lemon Avenue after work?"

"How about a little day-drinking?"

"I really need a drink."

The era of Nordstrom was the era of drinking and hangovers. The saying *work hard play hard* applied to working for that company. I can't think of one manager who didn't work at least a few shifts a month with a hangover from hell. Maybe it was the long hours. Maybe it was because we had to deal with customers and staff and more customers and have a tight fake smile all day. Whatever it was, we drank.

Gloria's, a Salvadorian/Mexican place, was our favorite. The margaritas had Everclear. The guac was delicious and happy hour ran long.

After an especially long night at Gloria's, I opened the

store the next morning with another employee. My eyes ached from lack of sleep and my mouth tasted like stale tequila and cigarettes, but I was there. I'd eaten four Altoids and it wasn't even ten a.m.

That's when she said, "Whew! Yasmin, did you have Italian last night? You smell like garlic."

I was horrified. Mornings from my freshman year of high school flashed through my mind. Because my mom had to be at work at six a.m., she'd drop me off at my best friend's house. His dad would drive us to school with the window of his pickup rolled down even in winter because he always smelled like garlic from the booze he drank every day.

I headed to the backroom, swearing I would take a break from drinking. In a week, though, the promise was forgotten as I raised an empty glass to the waiter and signaled for another.

Another sign I ignored was how I rarely visited El Paso. The longer and longer I stayed away, the further I got from home. I thought home was coming home to Drew, ordering Chinese takeout, and watching *Mad Men* together on the couch. I was away so long, I'd forgotten how home even felt.

"Lingerie, this is Yasmín, how can I help you?"

"Questashaciendo?"

"Excuse me?"

"Qué estashaciendo?"

"I'm sorry?"

"Se te acabó el español o qué?" The voice paused. "Mija, it's your mom."

"Oh! Mom!" I laughed. "I didn't recognize your voice."

I eyed the sales floor as if someone else could have heard the conversation. I didn't know what day it was in the stretch of days I'd been at the store. I often clocked in fifty-hour weeks in a light customer season. I felt so silly that I hadn't understood my mom. When was the last time someone had spoken Spanish to me? Ordering at Gloria's didn't count either.

When was the last time I'd spoken to my Ita?

TWENTY-SEVEN

WE FOUND OUT Ita died while at a Humperdinck's. Angie, my two-year-old niece Mica, and I had just left the hairdresser. We sat waiting for the waitress to take our drink order as we contemplated the platinum streak I'd just put in my black hair. I looked like a skunk, we agreed, when both our phones went off at the same time, a text from our mom, "Call me 911." We laughed and called fast to see who could get through first. I won. My mom answered. I barely heard her over the clangs and bangs of the restaurant. Angie's face was full of furrows and lines. I handed her the phone and gathered my niece. Angie started to cry.

The approaching waitress made an abrupt turn away from our table. I handed Mica to my sister and grabbed our bags. Outside, the bright afternoon sunshine seemed out of place. I glanced left and right, squinting hard against the light. A family walking in the door laughed. Mica cried. Her small body heaved with each breath. I walked steps behind my sister. The sunlight seemed to reflect off any metallic surface straight into my eyes. It felt like the time I tripped and crashed my head against the concrete step at my Ita's house.

"I just talked to her yesterday, and she sounded fine. Yesterday, she sounded fine." Angie jerked around to me, and Mica swung off her hip. "I just talked to her," she said over and over to me. I nodded. I hadn't spoken to her in months.

"Shut up!" my sister yelled at Mica as she tried to put her in the car seat, but Mica only wailed louder. Her face was so red it seemed it would pop. I stood to the side of the car, holding my bag, staring. Everything was moving too fast, and all I could do was get myself to Angie's purple mom van. Get in. Close the door. Sit.

I purchased plane tickets for my sister, my brother-in-law, and me. We flew on two different flights. One of Angie's biggest fears was a plane crash in which we all died, leaving my mom alone. She hates flying.

A friend, Mariah, took me to IHOP for breakfast before my flight. I attempted to eat, but the memory of countless breakfasts spent with my grandma proved too much. The waitress set down the eggs and bacon in front of me, but all I wanted were two eggs over medium, two corn tortillas, and three slices of muenster cheese, the way my grandma made them. She always asked what I wanted even though I wanted the same thing every morning. I remembered Rocío Dúrcal singing through fuzzy speakers in the background of the Saturday morning *Jetsons* cartoon as I waited for my breakfast. Lunch and dinner, I helped, but for breakfast she let me watch TV while she sang and cooked my eggs in our yellow kitchen.

I ran out of the IHOP. Mariah paid. If only I could have kept running. I struggled to keep my tears back. I'd cry later. I passed Love Field airport security and got on the plane in a haze. People kept their distance from me. I stared out at the world through my heavily tinted sunglasses, a shield for the remainder of my voyage home to El Paso.

The flight was the first time I had to think. I didn't have anything to do but wait. I tried to remember the last time we'd spoken—or I'd bothered to call—the last time I had come home to visit. I was always at work. I would call her later. I was tired. I was—and now there was no excuse. I didn't have to worry about making time. It had been made for me.

As we drove down Alameda Street to La Paz funeral home, I realized I hadn't been home to El Paso in two years. I looked for the store where Ita took me for *Tico Tico,* my favorite Mexican candy, a spicy, sugary chili powder, and corn on the cob with butter and chili powder. The stores was still there, but it looked different. The bright pink new, bu the poster board in the window that said "Elotes Preparados" was the same. I opened my mouth to ask Angie to stop but mashed my back against the furrow in the seat instead.

We parked and stood in front of the funeral home, the light bright in my eyes, the air warm even though it was September. Inside it was dim, cooler. As we walked into the small viewing room, panic bubbled up into my chest. My heart beat loudly in my ears and my whole body pulsed with the beat. I clenched my jaw and felt the urge to run away. There were no windows in the small, beige room, only dim fluorescent lighting that cast shadows across faces and corners that already hovered in darkness.

I willed my feet, lifting first right, then left, to move

forward. I knew I would regret not seeing her one last time before the cremation. My mom, Tío, Angie, and I were the only ones who were going to see her before it happened. My mom remembered Ita saying she didn't want to be buried, because the worms would eat her, and she didn't want anyone not from the family to see her dead. I smiled when my mom told us this. That sounded like my grandma, like her vanity. She wouldn't have wanted other people to see her dead or for someone else to have painted her up like a clown version of herself.

I saw us in memory as she lined the top lid of her eyes with black liquid liner and dabbed on pink lipstick. I was on the bed watching, waiting for her to get ready so we could leave. She would haunt us if we let someone else do her makeup.

I lingered behind my mom and uncle. My mom's back heaved up and down. A low unnatural sound, deep, like someone about to die, came from her. I stiffened, so rigid I thought I'd break if someone touched me.

My uncle sniffed and wiped at his cheeks with the palm of his right hand, his other hand rubbing my mom's back in a circle. They blocked my view. I stayed back, waiting for a sign that she was still going to look like *my* grandma. The soles of my shoes scratched against the thin carpet.

Then I moved forward, holding my breath. There was Ita—the sheet from her bed, white with little yellow and brown flowers, wrapped around her like a cocoon, a butterfly getting ready to fly.

I began to choke, my throat on fire. I willed myself not to run. Angie broke down beside me, crying, shaking my grandma: "Wake up, Ita! Wake up!" Her cries were magnified by the silence. I shrunk further inside myself, until everything was compacted so tight, it hurt to take a breath.

I reached out and smoothed my grandma's thin hair back, then touched the flattened bridge of her nose, broken in a fight. I traced the planes of her face. Her skin wasn't warm like it always had been when I was little, tucked beneath the heated nook of her arm. Her soft strong arms had always cradled me as we watched TV together.

My family faded into the background as I pictured her getting ready for bed for the last time, a nightly ritual I had seen countless times—she sang to herself, smoothed cream onto her face, pulled the flowered sheet around her, with only the murmur of the small radio on her nightstand as she quietly died alone.

TWENTY-EIGHT

THE THREE OF us—Mom, Angie, and I—sat at a Village Inn drinking coffee, looking at other people's obituaries, trying to figure out what to write. Since we'd never written an obituary before, we took bits and pieces from others' losses and made them our own.

We split up the list of things that needed to be done for the funeral. I found the urn online, an Asian-themed brass urn painted blue with gold etching. Ita liked Asian-themed items when she was alive, and I imagined her standing over my shoulder, pointing and saying "Esa, Prieta." My sister found the church, Holy Spirit of Hope, farther down on Alameda Street from the funeral home. My mom was still, waiting. I think she hoped she'd wake up and find everything was a dream.

As we drove down Alameda, I scrutinized the old buildings, faded bright pinks and greens, with hand-painted signs. The street smelled of used car lots and dark neighborhood bars. I'd fought to have her buried at the church we'd gone to when I was small, Sagrado Corazón in Segundo Barrio, but the church had refused. The Catholic Church doesn't approve of being cremated, an unnecessary burden while planning the service.

The service seemed like an afterthought. I'd said my goodbyes before she was cremated. The mass was for everyone else. The church was large and hollow, without stained-glass windows or alcove homes for the many saints Catholics prayed to. The altar was also bare, and it seemed strange to have the priest with all his layered gowns up there. It was bright and sunlight streamed through the smudged windows. Although the priest had been gracious and opened his church up to us, I couldn't help but think this wasn't the right place.

We stood—Mom, Angie, Tío, and his wife—in the front pew. My Aunt Sally, Tillie, and Uncle Feo, my grandma's siblings and their families, sat on the other side of the aisle. They asked, over and over, "Licha wanted to be cremated?" Her framed photo that we'd had enlarged sat on an easel near the altar. She was seventeen. It was before color film and slight touches had been applied, making her hair brown and her cheeks rosy. She looked the way she would have wanted to be remembered. How did they not know that?

People I didn't know came up to hug me. I pulled away as fast as I could, the curve of my body a question mark away from their open arms. I stiffened more and more each time and swallowed jagged edges of impatience as they whispered "I'm sorry" and "She loved you all very much." I choked back everything I wanted to say, words I knew wouldn't make a difference. Each breath I took in felt like a ribbon of words and sentences building inside of me, growing. I felt as if I could vomit all of them out on these strangers, these people who didn't know anything.

The smell of incense and candles took me right back

to Sunday church with Ita, when she scolded me for not wanting to shake hands. She would have scolded me now as I pulled away from their embraces.

The sermon started. I watched people's faces, somber, unsmiling, tears sliding down their cheeks. I didn't want to cry, not here. My mom sat beside me. She stared up at the cross on the wall with just one question on her face: "Why?" The priest allowed us to play some of my grandma's favorite music, Amalia Mendoza and Javier Solís, and my mom sang loud. Her voice was an anchor, low and heavy, and I felt myself sinking deeper next to her.

When it was time to give the host for the mass, my uncle stood, stiff, then turned back toward my mom. She just stared. My throat closed again, but I managed to whisper, "Do you want me to go, Mom?"

She nodded, silent.

I stood at the steps of the altar with my uncle, holding the dish of communion hosts. My jaw clenched at the familiar movement of people leaving the wooden pews and moving to form a line. Tío served the blood of Christ, cheap red wine in a gold-plated chalice he wiped and turned as people pressed their lips for a sip. "Peace be with you," I mumbled over and over as they took the small white circles and placed them in their mouths. "Peace be with you," as each person took a tiny piece of papery God. I glared at their solemn faces, gazing up, and wanted to yell, *"That's not God! He won't fill you!"* but instead I swallowed the words and nodded, silent, after each person, the dish cool against my hot, sweaty hands.

TWENTY-NINE

ITA'S HOUSE SAT in the middle of the block on California Street in the El Paso High area of El Paso. It was within walking distance of the Point, a tall copper-tipped stone obelisk overlooking the southernmost tip of the Franklin Mountains. Nestled in the armpit of the mountain were my schools: Lamar Elementary, Wiggs Middle, El Paso High.

My childhood was sprinkled around this red-brick Craftsman style home, with bits and pieces landing on each of its twenty-five stairs, leading up to the columns of the porch where I made crabgrass-filled mud pies and recorded myself singing "La Bamba."

Two years had passed since I'd last climbed these stairs. Now my legs trembled with each step until I reached the porch and leaned against the cement column. My mom fumbled with the many silver and gold keys on her key ring. *When was the last time she'd visited Ita?* Angie held the screen door open for her. I stayed back, not sure of what I would find inside, afraid of the smell.

Mom got the door open and we trickled in. I stood in the entryway breathing in a combination of outside air, dry and dusty, and inside air, scented with candle wax, sage incense, and mothballs. My footsteps creaked on the worn wooden floor, loud against the wordless silence. The room seemed the same, with its brown paisley couch and long green oval coffee table, the TV in the corner. But it also looked different, smaller. I stared at the large silver mirror over the fireplace and remembered how it had once seemed so high. Now I could see myself from the shoulders up. The sound of my niece Mica, running up and down the length of the dining room and living room floor, jolted me. The noise of her laughter and loud steps against the wood seemed out of place in the quiet of the house.

"Come here, mamita," Angie called, her arms out to pick Mica up.

The four of us stood between the two rooms, afraid to walk further, I suppose, because then we'd be closer to Ita's room. With each step, I took small, tentative breaths. I wanted the house to smell the same, without a hint of what had happened. I couldn't handle smelling her death. I needed to smell only the scents of a seventy-three-year-old's perfume, pungent, like flowers beginning to wilt.

My mom and sister walked into her room. I walked in last, placing my toe on the flattened green carpet as if testing the temperature of a pool. I couldn't just jump in. The bed was bare, with only the foam top liner. My mom sat. The mattress bowed in the center. I stood frozen in the doorway. It seemed wrong to sit on the bed where my Ita had died. Days ago, she'd gone to sleep and hadn't woken up. Her daytime caregiver came over as scheduled but found the screen door latched, no answer on the phone. My tío broke the latch and found her, lying facing up. He thought she was sleeping but saw her stillness, her chest no longer rising. He gave her CPR, and then smelled the exhaled breath, stale like dead flowers in week-old water.

My mom curled herself onto her side, knees pulled into her stomach like a child, and began to cry. Her tears washed away the violation I felt. My legs collapsed, the strings holding me up released. My sister sat on the end of the bed, her hand on my mom's shoulder, Mica quiet in her lap. Only sniffles filled the room until my mom rose from the bed, face red and pinched, and plopped down on the floor next to me, in front of the chest of drawers. My sister and I peeked at each other from across the room, then back at Mom as she pulled open the sock drawer. Pair by pair she squeezed the socks tight, making sure nothing was in them, until she'd made a mountain of socks.

"What should we do with these?" she asked.

The question hung in the air.

"We can make a donate pile and sell the things we think we can," Angie said, her voice high, each word a question in itself.

"Okay, whatever you girls think," my mom said, wiping at her cheeks.

Angie and I started cleaning the house out that day. We didn't know the whole process would end up taking two weeks. My mom faded into the background, watching my niece as we cleaned and separated Ita's life into piles. Room by room of the house's first floor: two bedrooms, laundry room, kitchen, bathroom, living and dining room. We played CDs of all her favorite music, Javier Solís, Amalia Mendoza, and Vicente Fernández.

Closets were filled with clothes from every era: wigs, shoes, coats, empty cream jars filled with jewelry, money hidden in the pockets of pants she hadn't worn in a decade. Behind the stove, we found a manila envelope with gold jewelry. In an eye shadow palette, we found an empty white envelope from the bank. We found old black and white pictures at the bottom of a closet, Styrofoam mannequin heads without wigs and faded faces, three never-opened cans of Lysol and empty yogurt containers. I never realized how much stuff she'd accumulated. I didn't understand why she kept most of it.

Many of the items had a story. These were the only moments when my mom's face seemed like her own, bright, caught in the memory playing in her mind.

"Mom, look at this dress!" I yelled out, holding a black dress with pink and purple flowers growing up from the bottom.

"I think there's a picture of your grandma wearing that dress somewhere." She peered around as if to find it. "I wore it when I was a teenager, I think—to a dance. I thought I looked hot!" She laughed, then stopped short as if she wasn't allowed to laugh.

"Hey, I wore that dress too!" Angie fingered the light chiffon fabric. "Ita let me borrow it. There is a picture."

"Cool! Can I have it?" I asked.

"Mija, you girls can take anything you want," she said squeezing Mica closer to her as she napped. "Your Ita would have liked it."

Later, I cleaned out the china cabinet filled with the same glasses and plates I'd cleaned as a little girl standing on a chair.

"She has so much stuff!" I said, pulling out the eighth

glass of a set.

"Ay, mija, your grandma was born in 1931, in the Depression, four of them with your aunts and uncle. They learned to use everything, not to throw anything away. Pobrecita de mi mamá, creció muy pobre."

The more we sorted and cleaned, the heavier the day got. I might as well have been carrying all the items we'd sorted on my back. I'd been with my family since I'd arrived but had texted on and off with one of my best friends, Nacho, who still lived in the city. One day I asked if he wanted to go to dinner. My grandma's house proved too much for me. Even though I didn't want to leave my family, I needed a break. I couldn't look at my mom anymore. She wasn't my mom right now, and I didn't know what hurt more, seeing her so broken or missing Ita.

I hadn't bothered to look at the check I'd signed when Nacho and I left Mesa Bar and Grill. The server had insisted each time he brought another bottle that it was their best. I giggled as I got into the cobalt blue Camaro. Tomorrow their best would be my worst. The leather scent of the car was still so fresh and new, I could still smell it after three and half bottles of Pinot Grigio. I kicked my heels off and tried to reach for the seat belt. I pulled, pulled again, but each time I got the belt to my chest, it stopped and jerked me back.

"You're pulling too hard, dude," Nacho said. He was driving.

"What? No, I'm not." I pulled again. "See!" The belt stopped halfway across my body.

Nacho sighed—he was my oldest friend, since the teen years when I was nothing more than a grungy little tomboy, trying to skateboard with the guys, going to class stoned after lunch, and scribbling Nirvana lyrics on everything I owned.

I jumped when I felt Nacho's hand reach across to buckle me in. I leaned back.

"Do you want to go somewhere else? Or are you done?" He cocked his head to the side, his hand resting on the gear stick. "I think you're pretty done, dude."

"I think we should go somewhere else." I clapped my hands. Then the thought of the morning—fast-approaching—stopped me. "No, wait. I think you're right. I think I'm done." A hiccup escaped. A period to my sentence. "I fuckin' hate the, *uupp,* hiccups. Can we get, *uupp,* water before you take me home?"

"Sure, dude, sure."

I leaned back and let the low rumble of the car rock me back and forth. I held my breath to stop the hiccups. The streetlights blurred and became connected lines. I leaned farther back into the seat, and turned toward the window, the seat belt cradling my face as he drove to the gas station.

"Any preference on what we listen to?" He pushed at his iPod.

"Whatever you want." I gulped another big breath of air, holding it.

When we stopped at a 7-11, I tried to find money inside my bag, a jumble of Camel Silvers, Orbit gum, my debit card, and my phone. I tried to hand my card to him, but he shook his head.

"Dude, I said you were done. I got it."

"But, I—"

He got out of the car. I leaned back again. My hiccups were gone. The bright lights from the store burned my eyes. I blinked as they watered. I reclined the seat, put my bare feet on the dashboard, and closed my eyes. I swallowed the fire in my throat and kept my eyes closed even though I knew it wasn't the lights anymore. I clenched my jaw and tasted the dry stale flavor of wine and too many cigarettes. I'd been trying to fight it, yet it rose from my stomach into my chest.

Angie and I had spent the day sorting my Ita's life into piles: donate, sell, trash. We'd thrown the makeup underwear away today. It brought back the memory of her wiping her face with them and the Olay cold cream. It seemed like it had just happened. I'd hoped each gulp of wine I took that night would dull that memory, but instead a sob escaped just as the door opened and Nacho returned. I snapped back against the chair.

"Did they have Smartwater?" I asked, putting my feet down.

Nacho stared at me. I grabbed the water from his hand. "Cool, thanks."

I took a long deep swallow, hoping he'd stop staring. But we'd been friends for too long for him not to notice the watery eyes. I sat in his car trying to fool him by taking deep swallows of water even though I was already drowning.

"I'm fine."

I couldn't meet his eyes. The sting hadn't faded. I reached for his iPod and scrolled through the playlists. "Here, I don't know what to play." I handed it back to him. "Hey, can we go to the park?"

I wanted to delay going back to my mom and sister as long as I could. There was a heaviness from everything. My sister and I were trying to take care of things in the house, but I felt like I couldn't breathe. I was suffocating. Tonight was just me trying to escape it, but who was I fooling?

"Really?" He paused without looking at me, iPod in his hand.

"I mean, we don't have to, that's cool." I shrugged. "Let's just go home."

I grabbed the water bottle, sat back, and turned toward the window again.

"Okay, we'll go to the park."

I pretended not to hear him sigh.

"How about some G&R?" he asked.

I nodded and put my feet back on the dashboard. The bass from the song started. We sang loud and out of tune.

Jungle, welcome to the jungle!

I sat up and jerked my head up and down, hair flying into my face. Everything spun, but I didn't care. For the first time in days, I couldn't hear myself think. I sang louder and louder. He drove even after we reached Madeline Park. He looped around and drove through the quiet hilly Kern Place neighborhood. Inside we sang. When the song finished, we looked up at each other and grinned. Big toothy smiles. I laughed and bounced in the seat, the seat belt restraining me.

"Again?" he asked.

"Yeah, can we?" I said, out of breath.

This time he picked Journey.

Just a small-town girl, living in a lonely world . . .

I started singing, but without the heavy bass reverberating through my body it didn't feel as good. I couldn't yell as loud. He kept singing, so did I, but I felt the clench of my stomach return and work its way up my chest. I looked at him and yelled.

"I just have to."

He stared at me, mouth open, mid-belting out. I turned the knob on the radio to the loudest and rolled down the window. I felt the cool breeze of the September night against my face and closed my eyes. I leaned out of the window as far as the door would let me, and I sang along, loud.

I unbuckled my seat belt, and Nacho grabbed at my left arm, but I shook my head. He hung on to me, looking back and forth between the winding street and me. I shook my head again and reached out. I pulled myself out of the window and sat on the window frame. I drummed my hands on the roof and laughed loud. The wind swallowed it. I'd managed to do it. He grabbed my left calf with his hand. I tried to hook my right foot underneath the seat.

The air was cold now, and it whipped my hair into my face and my mouth. I leaned back and moved my arms as if conducting my own orchestra. I heard the song and the wind. He drove. I felt free, and I gazed into the inky sky above us and laughed and laughed until I couldn't hide anymore.

I shuddered hard when the tears finally came. The sting hurt my eyes, and the wind dried them before they escaped. For days, I'd held it in. I'd tried not to cry as my family and I organized everything necessary for her funeral—answered the ringing phone at her house while we cleaned it out and swallowed each tear down until it felt like a hard pebble settled deep in my belly—but I was too full to be strong. I held the tears in because everyone else needed to cry. For days since I'd gotten the call that she'd died in her sleep, I hadn't cried. I'd booked a flight and had seen the faces of those around me crumble, but aside from escaped sobs, I'd swallowed everything. I couldn't hold it in any longer.

I opened my mouth and screamed. The air forced the sound back down into me, but I fought back, screaming even as my mouth dried and my lips stuck to my teeth. I screamed through the tears on my face and closed my eyes. My throat burned for a different reason now.

But still he drove. I screamed for all the memories we'd separated into piles today and for the makeup-stained underwear I'd wanted to keep but let fall from my hand into the large black trash bag. I tried to hear the words to the song I'd loved so much as a child, "*Yo ya me voy, a la tierra donde he nacido, para ver si así lo olvido . . .*" but they were just beyond my reach and I couldn't remember the rest of the words.

(This song is "Que mi Negra" but I don't know who sang the original version. I could only find banda versions in my search, which hurt me to listen to. So this time don't search for the song.)

I saw my grandma's petite figure as she made breakfast in her small yellow kitchen while my mom worked endless hours. I heard her singing the song I couldn't remember the words to now as we sat at The Tap with empty drinks in front of her and a basket of fries in front of me. I'd never really understood all the songs she sang as a child, but as these memories enveloped me, I let myself miss her. The burning feeling in her songs was the same one I had in my chest now.

My screams faded. I could only sob. I leaned against the cool roof of the car, my skin hot, and cried with my whole body. It was okay, only the night could see me.

We drove a little longer until Nacho tugged at my jeans. I knew it was time to go in. I slid back into the warmth and leather smell of the car. He pulled over at the park. I looked down at my hands and tried to wipe at the mingled tears and saliva. He handed me a napkin. The gesture made me sob again. I folded down into my lap. I cried into my jeans, covering my face for a while, until I felt his hand on my back. The warmth went through my thin blouse and I remembered where I was. I felt the curve of the leather seat against my back and the warm air from the vents against my cold skin. I took a deep breath, sat up, and blotted my face with the napkin. I stared out into the dimly lit green grass of the park.

"Can you take me home, please?" I asked, without turning my head.

I heard the movement of clothes scratching in the now quiet car. He began to reach across me for the seat belt.

"I got it," I said, leaning forward. He pulled his hand away. "I'm sorry. I mean I can do it now."

"Are you sure?" he asked.

I nodded, pulled on the belt, fastened it, sat back, and closed my eyes against the night.

The next day at Ita's, I had a three-and-a-half-bottles-of-Pinot Grigio hangover and lunch from Taco Tote. Still drunk, I ate with zeal, pouring red chile on my pork adobado taco. One hour in, in her pink bathroom, I hunched over red chile burning its way up my chest and into my mouth and nose, so dehydrated the chewed pieces of spicy meat lodged themselves in my throat. I coughed, eyes wet, the pain from the four days still worse than the food and bile heaving from my body. Afterward, I rinsed my mouth, my hands propping me up on each side of the sink, my face red and splotchy in the mirror, my eyes puffy and filled with tears. I closed my eyes, put my hands down, and turned away. I tried to sort through more things, but that day, I didn't have any fight left in me.

My mom convinced my sister to call it a day after I made two more trips to the bathroom. Walking to the car, my sister said, "Now we've wasted a day because you had to go out and party last night." I didn't respond, got into the passenger seat, and stared out the window through dark sunglasses. On the drive home, Angie pulled over twice for me to throw up. I stood on the side of the silver SUV retching, my whole body shuddering from the force, my eyes closed with each heave, my face red and tear-streaked when I got back into the car.

"Maybe you shouldn't drink for a while," Angie said as she patted my thigh. I nodded once, telling her I understood, and turned toward the window again.

A week later, I flew home to Dallas with a suitcase filled with Ita's dresses, blouses, perfume, jewelry. My sister stayed for another week to finish getting the house in order. At the El Paso airport, I hugged her tight for a long time. "I'm sorry I have to go back," I whispered in her ear.

Work wouldn't give me any more time off. I knew I was leaving her alone with my mom, who sat in a trance staring at memories no one else could see, and my tío, who had a pile of things in the corner of the living room he wanted but made excuses each time for why he couldn't take them. Riding the escalator up to security, I had the urge to run back and forget everything, my job, my apartment—leave it all, the force so strong my stomach turned and knotted—but I stared forward, unblinking, my feet anchored to the metal staircase propelling me away. The memories of my Ita lay sorted into stacks of things all through her house. I carried as many as I could with me—down the twenty-five concrete stairs onto California Street, past Brown Street, and away from El Paso High and my childhood.

THIRTY

BEING IN EL Paso for two weeks, then returning to a bed I'd missed in Dallas, was jarring. The whitewashed version of my life resumed where it had left off, but a large black suitcase sat in the corner of my second-floor bedroom, unpacked, holding in the smells of home: gardenia and Avon bath oil. A week after I was back, I had my first dream about my grandma.

I sat with my great Aunt Tillie at a round cherry-red table that had overstuffed black barstools. I scanned the people around me, their bright clothes, the speakers playing "Young at Heart." I'd just popped into a Rock Hudson movie, bright Technicolor reds, blues, and yellows everywhere. The bar was all streamlined clean lines and minimalist designs, and I expected to see Bobby Darin splish-splashing among the crowd with a remote that could control everything from lighting to pouring my next vodka tonic. I was in awe.

My aunt was talking. I saw her glossy red lips moving, but I didn't hear a word. I kept looking around, scanning faces, searching for someone, but I just didn't know who. The urge to move, to find what I was looking for, traveled up my silver strappy-heeled feet to my chest, where I felt a pull from an invisible string. Like a puppet, I got up, leaving my aunt midsentence in a conversation I hadn't heard. I waded through groups of people—talking, laughing, martinis in hand—toward the bar. I looked down at the bright sapphire dress I wore and found something familiar in the large round buttons. I fingered them, felt the thick, glossy plastic, trying to remember where I'd seen them before, a tickle in my memory, when someone bumped me from behind. I turned, trying to find where the elbow had come from, when I saw a face I'd only seen in photos: my grandma, younger than I'd ever seen her, smiling at me from across the bar.

My hand fell away from the button: the string at my center pulled me toward her. She didn't seem to move, but the harder I tried to get to her, the farther away she got. The crowd of charcoal gray suits and pink-manicured hands holding drinks doubled in front of me. The music changed. "Shake, Rattle and Roll" spilled from the speakers, louder. The hard beat made everyone shimmy and shake. I saw the top of the black dress Ita wore, a glass in her black-gloved left hand, her hair dark and in a sleek chignon high on her head, an image I'd seen many times in photos.

I pressed against the people dancing in front of me. They were oblivious to the elbows and shoulders I shoved against them. They just kept right on shaking and wiggling, smiles large and toothy even as I pushed with all my weight. I tried to reach Ita but couldn't make any progress. The Technicolor people jammed against me, swallowing me with their thick polyester fabrics and glossy smiles, faster, all going against the direction I was heading in.

She smiled, shiny red lips, nodding me on, but I couldn't

reach the face, the body I wanted to hold in my arms. The harder I fought—pushed, shoved, stepped on, elbowed—the farther away she moved. I heaved. My body was pulled in one direction but shoved in another. I stared, eyes wide, as the crowd began to swallow her. My throat constricted, and my chest tightened. I couldn't breathe, but I cried her name out, strangled against the people multiplying between us. She only waved at me with her gloved hand and smiled. I woke with tears stinging my eyes.

THIRTY-ONE

I WOKE UP hungry, a deep hunger down in my belly. It called for a mental flip of a Rolodex of meals. I hoped I'd find what I craved. I raced through my morning ritual of brushing my teeth, washing, and coiffing my hair. I paused in front of the white bathroom mirror. "*Today is going to be a good day. Today is going to be a good day. Today is going to be a good day.*" This mantra had become a necessity six months ago. Each word came out with an exhaled breath, fell into the sink, and circled the drain.

On the way to work, I settled on an Asiago cheese bagel. As I chewed, I lingered over the bready, moist ball, moving it around in my mouth, savoring it.

At lunch, I was still hungry—a shrimp po'boy sandwich . . . no, chicken pomme frites. I dined instead on a luscious meal of creamy Yukon gold potato jalapeño soup, each spoonful dissolving on my tongue, the salad of tequila lime shrimp savory, plump, exploding in my mouth. I felt content, a silence in my body with my stomach full. Until I got back to work.

I forced a smile the rest of the afternoon and gave verbatim answers to shopping customers. I gave a toothy smile to Lexi, a coworker who made comments as if speaking to herself, "I hate this paper!" as she pulled at a receipt roll. Then she asked in a sugar-laden voice, "Don't you hate this paper?" I pretended not to hear. "Well, don't you hate it, Yasmin?" I hoped my gritted teeth passed for a smile.

At dinner, I made Ita's tacos, humming quietly as I cooked, thankful she had shown me how to cook them. Ground beef and potato seasoned in a way only she could have taught me, a fried hard shell, layered with Muenster cheese, crisp lettuce, a firm tomato wedge, a white onion sliver, and red chile de árbol salsa. I chewed, letting each bite take me back to the memory of the small yellow kitchen where we had eaten together when she was alive.

"I've been so hungry!" I said to Ita. "But I don't know what I want."

I watched her cook, refrying beans with cheese in a heavy black pan, only her back visible, her reddish-brown hair in a French twist held together by numerous bobby pins.

"Nothing sounds good," I complained, arranging salt and pepper shakers and other condiments in the center of her plastic yellow-flowered tablecloth.

"¡Tienes hambre de Dios!" her voice sang out operatically as she eyed me with her left brow kissing her hairline.

When she said this, I'm not sure if she meant we had a hunger for God or for religion. Either way, I needed something.

"Ay, Ita! No, I want something good. *Food* good."

Now, back in my own kitchen so very far away from that memory, my laugh echoed in the empty space. Whenever I was hungry for something, but didn't know what, Ita had said that. I never understood what hambre de dios meant. I heard her voice singing out in my mind "¡Tienes hambre de Dios!" as I reached for another taco. Then another.

Days after the tacos, I continued to eat everything I encountered. I felt like an automatic gun, taking out everything in my sights. I ate butterflied garlic bread with pasta al dente in a crème sauce, the richness satisfying the growing, empty ache inside me. I ate Skittles and Starbursts, hoping the sticky sugar would nauseate me into submission. I ate a greasy Jumbo Jack from Jack in the Box at two in the morning and a thick, creamy spoon of peanut butter in my kitchen at seven a.m. I pressed it against the roof of my mouth and let the clump dissolve, staring out my kitchen window at the darkened Dallas skyline. The moments before it melted away, I felt my chest relax. Then the tightness I had become accustomed to returned.

I went to the grocery store and ate while I shopped. A man stopped to ask me if I would be paying for the eaten apple, pear, and candy bar. I raised my eyebrows and inspected the cart filled with a rotisserie chicken, Lays, Wholly Guacamole, bloody ground beef and asked, "What do you think?" I opened my mouth. Melted chocolate not yet swallowed showed him a gooey spider web there to trap more food. Each time I ate, I heard my Ita's voice: "¡Tienes hambre de Dios!"

Weeks went by, and the hunger would not abate. I only felt the breath move quickly in and out of my body when I was eating. Desperate to stop, I went to the first church I saw. "¡Tienes hambre de Dios!" I heard again as I walked into the stained-glass cathedral. I took a deep breath, knelt and crossed myself as I'd been taught. I waited for the calm I needed to overcome me. I smelled the familiar scent of candle wax and incense, and remembered sitting in a similar church in a similar pew a long time ago.

We went to Spanish mass every Sunday without fail. Every time the mass got to the handshaking portion, I leaned toward my grandma. "Ita, I don't want to shake people's hands," I whispered, wiping my damp palms on my jeans.

"Tienes que," she hissed back, "¿No le darías la mano a Diosito?"

I wrinkled my nose. *No, maybe I wouldn't shake Diosito's hand.* I slouched, my ten-year-old body trying to hide amongst the unbending pews, and stared down at my scuffed Vans, cheeks hot with shame. When everyone stood to shake hands, I bent over and began to fiddle with my shoelaces. Ita elbowed me in the side.

"Que la paz esté contigo," I mumbled as strangers' hands grasped my palm and squeezed. "Peace be with you."

The two minutes felt longer than the mass. Ita turned at me and smiled as if to say, "¿Ves?" with her eyebrow raised.

You see?

But now, I sat staring at the empty seat beside me. There was no one to scold me about not wanting to shake Diosito's hand. There was no one—only me—so I waited, prayed, for the hunger to subside, but it only seemed to worsen. My stomach's growls were a crescendo, my insides twisting and turning in on themselves. My stomach contorted into knots, and a hunger pain wrenched through me so strong I doubled over. I felt lost in the pew shadows as I gazed up at

Jesus with his open arms.

He seemed like a crystallized icon inviting me in. I was the only one among rows of chocolate pew bars and candied icons tempting me to take a bite. My cheeks burned, the flush crept down my body as I leaned forward, teeth sinking in, and I bit, hard. I rolled the rich, smooth flavor along my tongue, a waterfall down to my hot center with each cool bite extinguishing the burn of my mouth, my chest, my stomach. I couldn't stop. It hurt too.

Before I knew what was happening, I was eating the pews. Then I ate St. Michael and St. Lazarus. I walked up to God and broke off his opened palmed hand and bit his thumb, the lightness of pound cake and the smooth, creamy flavor of tiramisu. I sank to my knees. God tasted better than anything I'd ever had. I ate and ate and ate until I thought I could eat no more. I finished God and went to the windowpanes made of spun sugar. I ate the confessional box, and the combination of dark chocolate and nuts almost had me, but still, I kept eating.

I kept eating until there was nothing left but a dog-eared black leather Bible in my mouth, the pages folding back like layers of a light pastry turnover. Finished, I sat on an empty lot, my stomach swollen and distended. Just when I thought I was satisfied, I felt a tremble rise from my toes into my chest and into my throat, and my mouth opened. A great burp escaped as well as a burning heave making my eyes water and sting. A piece of soggy dog-eared Bible landed in front of me on the dirty floor, half-chewed. I gazed at the mutilated flaky pages, then up, eyes damp, at the darkened sky, absent of stars.

THIRTY-TWO

FOR NINE YEARS, I worked around boobs. From Victoria's Secret to Neiman's to Nordstrom, I had been fully invested in the corporate culture. But then there was a shift in me. I didn't realize it, but people around me did. After my grandma's death in late 2007, everything was different. My world had been turned upside down. The constant guilt I tried to hide hung around me like a never-ending hangover. Six months after Ita died, when the economy slumped in 2008, my investment in this life also took a downward turn.

Every month, all the Nordstrom stores came together for a rally. They were like high school pep rallies for grown adults. I studied the audience and small stage they set up for the events. We were like slices of pie, each group set up under large signs with their store numbers: 720, 723, 722, etc. We all stopped chatting and focused on the stage when a crackle came through the speakers.

At this particular store rally, the higher-ups were really laying it on thick. They were trying to inspire all the department managers to make their sales goals. It worked on everyone, I think, except me. Then the crackle stopped and a voice I'd heard before sounded through the third floor of the store. It bounced off hard plastic mannequins dressed in expensive outfits, off shiny sales fixtures filled with high-priced items, and into our ears.

"We choose to go to the moon. We choose to go to the moon in this decade and do the other things, not because they are easy, but because they are hard, because that goal will serve to organize and measure the best of our energies and skills, because that challenge is one that we are willing to accept . . . "

When the JFK clip finished, someone important got on stage and talked about meeting our sales goals, raising UPTs (units per transaction), beating LY (last year's numbers), and on and on. He told us the financial challenges we were facing were just like the impossible goal of going to the moon, and if we could get to the moon, we could make our sales goals.

I scrutinized the faces wearing MAC makeup and Chanel lip gloss and Burberry ties and how their gaze was transfixed on the short stocky man speaking on stage. Was I the only one who saw something wrong with comparing the race to the moon with selling high-priced lingerie that most people didn't need?

Were they fucking serious?

I stayed another year even after that stupid rally. That was a bit longer than my sister, who'd already moved back to El Paso. My Ita's death was a signal for us, I think, to come home. To reevaluate. To focus on what was important. Prada wasn't sexy at all anymore. I had a closet full of designer clothes and sunglasses, but that was no longer satisfying. Aside from brief highlights, my days were all exactly the same. I didn't get a rush from having a big sale anymore. I was tired of working fifty-plus-hour weeks and going to work hungover at least once a week.

Because, after my Ita died, that got even worse.

I'm sure there are a lot of other things I'm forgetting. Although I was doing an okay job, my heart wasn't in it anymore. The only time I perked up was when I helped women with prostheses. Only then did I feel like I was doing something worthy. Important. Someone else could have done better at the other stuff. Selling expensive items to people was not important to me. I was tired, but I was also scared.

My epic meltdown came after getting written up at work. I followed this with a long night of drinking and chunks of my evening missing. I don't remember how I got home because my car wasn't outside. I also don't remember why I called my sister. Even my most drunken brain knows better. That night, all bets were off. To this day, I don't know what I said, but it worried my sister enough that what seemed like moments later there was a knock on my door and my friend Mariah was there. I tried to get her to leave. I yelled at her. I think I tried to punch her. Drinks with friends had always been about having fun, a party, but now it had turned into something ugly. I had turned into everything I hated.

After some much-needed vomiting, I sat on the floor of my bathroom with Mariah, trying to piece things together.

"But what happened?" she asked.

I didn't know how to respond. I really didn't know what happened. That day at work, the store manager had called me into her office. She wrote me up for leaving at five on a day we'd had an event even though I'd been there before the sun rose. Apparently a ten-hour shift hadn't been enough. I'd left at the end of my shift with my assistant manager there to close. When I'd tried to explain that, the store manager had just furrowed her brow and pushed the writeup toward me. I'd gone straight to a bar after.

"I'm just tired. I'm tired of all of it."

I didn't know it then, but the timing of everything, the write-up, calling my sister, even the wicked hangover were all the best things that could have happened because they forced me to leap.

I worked the afternoon shift the next day. Before going in, I called my sister in tears. I finally broke down and admitted how unhappy I was with work, my life, and the direction it was heading in. Angie listened and told me what I needed to hear.

"Come home."

At first, I thought she was being silly. *How could I just quit my life in Dallas?* What would I do back in El Paso? I took a shower and tried to wash the smell of Jäeger and smoke off my skin and hair.

Could I quit and just go home?

Once I began to entertain the idea, things fell into place in a short couple of hours. I called Angie and asked her what graduate programs UTEP offered. She called me back minutes later.

"They have an MFA program in Creative Writing. Isn't that what you wanted?"

"When is the application deadline?"

"January. You can still apply."

I hung up. I stood in the steamy bathroom, wrapped in a towel, not knowing what to do with the information she'd just given me. My eyes were bloodshot, and my throat was hoarse from vomiting the night before, but I felt something I hadn't felt in a while. Hope.

I stared in the mirror, turned away, picked up my phone and dialed my townhome's leasing office.

"Hi, I just renewed the lease a couple days ago, and I was wondering if I would be able to break it without a fee? Is that possible?"

I waited as the woman looked up my name and lease information. I didn't know what I wanted her response to be.

"Miss Ramirez?"

I held my breath.

"I wouldn't normally do this, but it's just two days since you renewed. If you've changed your mind, I can easily put it in the shredder."

No matter how many times I tell the story, it sounds like something made up, but it isn't. I'm not that good of a writer. I had been fighting so hard that I think once I stopped fighting, everything fell into place. I was meant to come home.

My mouth opened. "Yes, please. I don't want to renew. Thank you."

I called Angie from the Starbucks parking lot before my shift. I was going to be late, but I didn't care anymore. I stared into the mirror on my sun visor waiting for her to answer. My giant dark Valentino sunglasses hid my eyes, but that haggard pale face was still visible. I took a sip of the coffee and sighed.

"What did your complex say?"

She didn't even say hello. I swallowed.

"Can you do me a favor? Can you write my letter of resignation and email it to me?"

"Wha—yes!" she practically shouted. "I'll do it right now. I'll text you when I send it."

"Wait—"

"Yeah?" She paused.

"Thanks, Ang."

I peered into the mirror one more time and took a deep breath. I had one more call to make.

"Mom?"

"How are you, mija? Your sister told me—"

I didn't want to talk about last night.

"Mom . . . can I come home?"

THIRTY-THREE

THE FIRST WEEKS of being back in El Paso were weird and surreal. I was home, but it wasn't the home I remembered. I'd been gone almost ten years. Businesses I'd used as landmarks were gone and a whole new highway had popped up in the Far Eastside. I also didn't know anyone anymore.

My mom had gotten married while I was away, to nice man, Joe, who opened his home to me, but this made things even more surreal. For some reason, when I called Mom that day in the car, I thought I would be returning to our house on the East side. That's silly to think that things would have stayed the same from when I left a decade ago, but I think that's what I was craving. I didn't need a house full of things. I'd had that in Dallas. I needed a home. *My home.*

Both Mom and Angie were over the moon to have me back. Although sometimes I caught them looking at me with concern shadowing their eyes.

"You can't work for at least a month."

That's what Mom told me once I'd put my stuff in a storage unit and unpacked what I needed into the bedroom I now had at her and Joe's house.

"A month?"

She nodded. "Yes, I don't know what that place did to you, but you're not yourself. A month."

From the set of her mouth, I knew there was no changing her mind. At first, it was great. I slept for what seemed a hundred years. I was so tired, I became like Drew. I slept, woke up, ate, then slept again. Drew was very happy about this and cuddled at my feet or by my side. I read. I watched TV I don't think I left their house for over a week.

The first day I did leave, I took my car for an oil change. At the register, when the attendant asked my name, I responded slowly with, "Yas-mean. Y-a-s-m-i-n. Rah-mir-ez. R-a-m—"

He was staring at me with his mouth open. In Dallas, I always had to say my name slowly and phonetically, or else both my first and last name were mispronounced. Here, well, maybe he needed help with Yasmín, but definitely not my last name. My cheeks burned. I scurried to a seat in the waiting area and hoped no one else had heard.

Next I drove to the grocery store for tomatoes. I love tomatoes, and since I was a little girl, I'd slice them up, sprinkle them with salt and pepper, and eat them just like that. At the Big 8 market I went to, they only had Roma tomatoes, not hothouse. I left the store in a huff, went back to my Mom's, and cried. When I tried to explain to her about the tomatoes, she just stared at me for a moment from the doorway of my bedroom.

"I can't even find my tomatoes here!" I cried.

My mom sat on the bed next to me, "Mija, it's going to take some time. Just give it time. You need to relax. You don't know how to relax anymore."

"But what about my tomatoes?" I asked, wiping my cheeks.

She smiled. "We'll find the tomatoes."

A few days later, I joined a gym. I needed to do something, move, go places. I felt—I don't know what—but I'd napped all the naps I had in me. So I started to clean. A deep clean where I took everything out of their kitchen cabinets and wiped the shelves down. I alphabetized Mom's books and DVDs. I wiped down the walls in the living room and hung family pictures they left sitting on coffee tables. Drew watched from whatever nearby perch she found. Joe was not a fan of cats, but she seemed to know this and didn't leave the hall that led to my bedroom.

I tried job searching against Mom's wishes, but that created a whole other anxiety attack. Most of the jobs were in the service industry or retail. The thought of working on a sales floor again, much less at a place like Dillard's or Macy's, made my stomach and throat contract with dread.

"I thought I told you not to work," Mom said from the kitchen counter.

I sat at their oval kitchen table while she made beef flautas. It had held familiar stacks of mail up until a few days ago, before I'd cleaned it off. Now I sat criss-cross applesauce on one of the chairs and watched as Mom cooked. I didn't even remember my mom making flautas before, but she was doing everything in her mom powers to make sure I felt comfortable in her house. In El Paso.

"Mom, but what am I going to do? My savings are gonna run out. You can't support me forever."

I pushed my choppy chin-length hair back. It was holding strong, but I knew I would have to find someone who could cut my hair, and I was worried. People who knew how to cut short hair in El Paso had been scarce when I was younger. From the moments I'd been out of the house, things seemed the same. Long hair everywhere.

"Didn't you come home to go to school? Go to school then," she said, rotating the flautas in the hot pan.

I rolled my eyes. I suddenly felt sixteen again.

"I can't just go to school." I threw my hands in the air. "I have to get accepted in the program."

My mom studied me and shrugged. "Just look. Nada se pierde en ver."

So I looked on the UTEP website and found that I could take some graduate level courses without being in a program. I just had to be non-degree seeking. Turns out Mom was right. I didn't lose anything by looking. So I went through the application process and registered for a food and culture class in the English department. I had no idea what that meant, but it was starting in a few weeks.

The next months were very disorienting. I hadn't been in school in five years, and now I sat in a room of graduate students all saying things I didn't understand.

"The cultural implications of a meal are far beyond the understanding—"

"Doesn't it go to show that the act of breaking bread has a much deeper meaning on how one shares and consumes—"

I scanned the room and felt like an imposter. I'd never stopped reading. I read a lot, but I read fiction. Some romance, but generally literary fiction. My friends in Dallas thought I was crazy when I tried to tackle a list of the best hundred books ever written. I only got about thirty in, but still, all that reading had not prepared me for what was being said in this room.

Reading food theory dumbfounded me. The professor, Dr. Meredith Abarca, spoke so passionately about food, my cheeks flushed. I don't think I'd ever felt so passionately about anything in my life, so I read the assigned readings, did the homework, went to class, but was often mute in class for fear of saying something silly. I kept my head down until Dr. Abarca called on me one day.

"You, what do you think?"

I kept scribbling in my notebook. I figured if I always looked like I was writing, she would never call on me.

"You." I glanced up. "Yes, you. What do you think?"

My pen stopped. I peered into her face, a messy halo of dark hair, and opened my mouth.

THIRTY-FOUR

THAT FOOD AND CULTURE class was the start of a new chapter for me. Little did I know a few years after I'd be cooking a meal with my boyfriend for my family.

I spent the morning dry-rubbing cumin, salt, and cayenne on raw racks of red, fleshy ribs. Chopping firm mangoes, cucumbers, and sharp-smelling cilantro. The avocados, I realized, were too firm and we had to go get more. We couldn't have a barbecue without guacamole. Everyone was coming over: my mom, my sister, their husbands, Tío, and my two small nieces, Mica and Ale. It was going to be a full house in this small apartment on Arizona Street.

My grandma had run the small house as a duplex when she was alive. Now my mom was the landlady. Daniel, my boyfriend, who I'd met in my MFA program, had moved in a month ago. He'd invited my family over. In preparation, we'd executed our well-choreographed cooking dance. I looked forward to asking them more questions about my grandma, to help fill in the holes in all the pieces I was writing. I also really looked forward to feeding them.

After a bumpy start, everything had fallen into place with school. Dr. Abarca's class had renewed my love for food and cooking. I basked in memories of cooking with Ita. I'd even started writing about her after a short piece about Ita taking off her makeup had wowed the class. I hadn't planned on writing about her. It had just happened.

"Do you need something?" Daniel asked.

"Nope," I answered, chopping white onions for the guacamole. "Do you want to start the fire?"

"Yeah, I need a fire," he opened his tanned arms wide, "for all this food."

As we prepped, my relatives arrived: my sister's group, my mom's, then finally my tío. We all stayed in the kitchen around the table, around the food, pushing dishes against one another. Each group brought something with them: more beer, more food, more ice. Guacamole, chile con queso, tostadas, pinwheels, mango-cilantro salsa, cheesy refried beans, all packed Tetris-like, waiting to be scooped and dipped.

The smell of the grill drifted in as Daniel and I moved back and forth between alternating trays of cooked kabobs and raw ribs, grilled asparagus with drumsticks. The background to all the conversation and laughter: a playlist of Amalia Mendoza songs that I'd created when I started writing stories about my Ita in earnest. The station helped jog my memory. (Search for Amalia Mendoza's "Mucho Corazón" and Javier Solís's "Payaso" to listen to while you read.)

It put me back in the small yellow kitchen with her while we cooked.

"Mom, Mom, Mom!" I called out over everyone's chatter.

Mica and Ale ran up and down the small hallway, their

steps echoing loud on the old wooden floors.

"Mama! Mica! Mama, don't run!"

Di si encontraste en mi pasado. The music went through the house.

"Mom!"

"What, mija?"

"Don't run! Go play in the living room!"

Pides cariño, pides olvido . . .

"Do you need something to drink? Another Coke?" I pointed at her half-empty glass.

"I'd like another Coke," said Joe, her husband.

"With ice?"

Pero mucho corazón . . .

"Mommy, I need to go to the bathroom. Mommy, I need to go to the bathroom. Mommy, I need to go to the bathroom."

"Ask your Tanti."

"Yes, please, mija."

Una razón para quererme . . .

"Tanti, can I use your bathroom, please?"

"Yeah, mama, it's in the hallway. Do you need help?"

Even though she swung her head from left to right, I walked her toward the bathroom.

"Do you want me to stay?"

"No, Tanti," she said, shaking her head again as she tugged at small buttons with her small, pudgy hands.

I smiled and closed the door. Little people with such attitude already. What would she be like later? Like me? I turned, pausing outside the door, wondering if, when I came back, I'd find a small toilet-paper mummy with her pants down.

No necesito una razón Me sobra mucho, Pero mucho corazón . . .

The small hallway connected the living room to the kitchen but was dim and wide enough for me to stand unseen and breathe for a moment to just listen to everything my family said. It was a small moment of quiet. I breathed deeply, inhaling the smell of grilling meat and love.

"Ale, are you done, mama?" I asked into the door just as she was pulling it open. She gazed up at me, her eyes taking up most of her face. "Yes, Tanti. I go to the bathroom myself now," she said again, her head bobbing up and down.

I pressed my lips together and nodded back, my eyes wide and unblinking as hers. Just as I was about to smile, she ran off to the living room. "Mica, that's my toy!" I stepped toward the inevitable argument and tears but changed my mind and turned back toward the kitchen. My sister could deal with them. I stifled a giggle as I heard, "Mommy! Ale took my toy."

Payaso con careta de alegría . . .

"Is everyone okay? Do you guys need anything?"

"No, no, mija. Sit. You've been running back and forth." My tío patted the chair next to him. "How've you been, mija?"

"Good, Tío, busy, writing, school, you know? Trying to finish."

"I almost thought I should wear a tie, since you invited me to Daniel's house," he said, wiggling his eyebrows up and down.

"Ay, Tío." I turned toward my mom and rolled my eyes.

"How are the stories about your Ita coming along?"

Soy un triste payaso . . .

"They're coming"—I reached for a beer from the cooler—"but it's hard deciding what to write about, you know?"

"I have tons of stories about your Ita, mija, if you need any ideas. Sis, do you remember when Moms and I used to go to Juárez? She'd fall asleep on the way back, and I'd wake her so she could say, 'American.'" He crinkled his chin to his chest and slurred his words.

"Uh huh, you two would get plastered," my mom said, nodding.

"Just them two? Huh?" Angie said, bobbing her head on her shoulders just as Ale had earlier. "I remember when you and Ita used to go out partying on New Year's and bring me back the little party favors."

"Ay, Angelica, that's because it was New Year's."

"Yeah, New Year's." Tío wiggled his eyebrows again.

"You and Ita used to go party a lot too," Angie said again, chin jutting out past her body at Mom.

"I'm not writing about Ita and Mom going partying!" I said before Angie's and my mom's heads met in the middle of the room like two angry bobble heads.

"Oh," Angie dipped a tostada in the refried beans, "what about when Salvador tried to kill Ita?"

"Her second husband . . . after she'd divorced the donor," my mom added.

I turned to Angie, eyebrows crinkled.

"Their dad," Angie said.

"Why not just say Dad?"

"Because he was *just* the donor." My mom shook her head.

"I say *my dad* even if he wasn't around," I said, eyes squinted.

"*Anyway* . . ." Tío interrupted, "your mom and I were just kids when Salvador tried to kill Moms."

"Ita's fatal attraction. He broke out of jail after he'd murdered a man, shot him in the back of the head. Your Ita filed for divorce while he was in jail—he could have killed my mom. Somehow, she ran out, carrying me, pulling your uncle to the police outside, because by then they'd shown up. In the cop car, I was so scared, I peed on my mom."

I tried to imagine my mom as a four-year-old clinging to her mom while shots were fired at Salvador.

"He always told my mom, she would only be his," Mom said, but her gaze was somewhere far away.

"When I was making the family tree, I found the newspaper article from the shootout," Angie added. "There's a picture of my little Ita with rollers in her hair."

"Your grandma . . . she was one tough woman," my tío said. "She didn't take crap from no one. When I was little, some boys picked on me, and she taught me how to fight. She told me, 'Nunca busques pleito, pero no te dejes' and no one picked on me after that."

"Yeah, Ita did that with me too." I nodded, remembering when I learned to throw a punch, my fist slapping against the palm of her hand.

"She worked hard, my mom, to support your uncle and me." My mom nodded, her eyes still cloudy. "But I think she would have been happier if she'd been able to keep all of us."

"Nine of us, right, sis?"

Daniel walked into the room with a tray full of glossy barbecue ribs, and the room fell silent.

He looked around, started to back up, then glanced at

the ribs in his hands.

"Anyone want ribs?" he asked.

I jumped up and grabbed the tray from him. "Thank you! We were wondering what was taking so long."

"Yeah, mijo," my mom chimed in, "we thought you were eating all the ribs out there."

"Yeah, mijo, did you go kill the cow?" Tío added.

The girls ran into the kitchen from the living room. "Mommy, we're hungry!"

Daniel stared at me, his dark brown eyes asking if everything was all right. I nodded. I held the tray out as my family reached for smoky ribs. We all started talking at once, laughing and asking what had happened to the music.

Everyone found a chair and nibbled, each of us working to keep our mouths full of the darkened edges of the meat, crusted with seasoning.

THIRTY-FIVE

SATURDAY MORNING, I woke, sunlight streaming in through white plantation blinds, my eyes sleep-crusted. I rested my elbows on my knees, fingers pushing at the hair in my face, swallowing at a lump lodged in my throat. It was as stubborn as me. The fading dream eased the ache in my chest, but, like the light, it still peeked through the cracks.

"Are you hungry?" Daniel's deep voice interrupted my quiet.

I looked up. He stood in the doorway, tall, bed-headed, waiting for an answer. My mouth opened to tell him about the dream, but I couldn't form words—they were trapped below the growing lump. I shook my head. His steps, retreating on the tile floor, echoed. I exhaled, the breath finding its way around the unmoving curved edges of my throat. I knew he'd still make enough breakfast for two. That would give me a chance to piece the dream together and find the right words to explain a wound I didn't even understand.

Drew meowed as I walked past her and the tangled gold comforter on the floor. In the bathroom, I locked the door and stood with hands braced on the cold white porcelain sink. I exhaled, long, from deep in my belly. Three years later and the dreams still came: some good, some bad. Today's had been good, but still a punch in the stomach unable to break apart the lump of guilt.

I took a deep breath and relived the dream again, then shoved it down inside me with the rest of them.

In the dream, I sat at dinner with friends laughing when my phone rang. The display screen said, "Ita." I swallowed and answered.

"Hello?"

"¿Cómo está mi Prieta?" Her voiced crackled with laughter.

"Who is this? It can't be you, Ita. You're dead." I gawked. Panic bubbled up. My friends at the dinner table kept talking and laughing. The colors of the restaurant began to blend together.

"No más te quería decir, Prieta, que te quiero mucho, ¿eh?"

"Ita? Ita, is it you? How is this you?" I woke up seconds later.

Now I stood barefoot in the bathroom, tears dropping from my flushed cheeks into the sink, willing my memory not to forget her words.

Psychologists theorize that everyone is your dreams is a version of your subconscious. Fuck that. Even in death, my Ita takes care of me. Whenever I need her, even when I don't know I do, she visits me. She tells me she loves me. She reminds me that I need to forgive myself.

THIRTY-SIX

QUEEN BEDROOM FURNITURE set with mattresses, a dining room table, a twin bed

The summer of 2015, Angie and I cleaned out my mom's storage unit. It only took eight years after my Ita's death for us to convince Mom to let us take "some" things out. My mom borders on being a hoarder. She doesn't want to let go of things because they remind her of Ita. I'm the same: I don't want to stop writing about Ita. My hoarding just takes up less space.

frame my dad made me, a 55-gallon fish tank, a 150-gallon fish tank, two stair steppers

Shortly after I moved to Dallas to live with Angie and go to college, my mom married Joe. We'd never met the guy. She just called to tell us she was married. My uncle packed up her house, put everything in storage, and moved into the house while she moved in with Joe. Five years later, after my Ita died, Mom just kept adding to the unit. All the things she didn't want to be bothered with were put there to be covered by years of desert dust.

several karate gi, two elliptical machines, two weight benches, four boxes of kitchen items, a box of

When we first rolled up to the grimy, once-white aluminum door, we thought we knew what to expect. We arrived under the pretense that Angie was going to use a baker's rack at her house. But really, we were executing a plan we'd been working on for the last year to clean out the storage unit once and for all. I had three weeks off before the summer semester class I was teaching began, and Angie had a month off before starting her new nursing job. We knew our mom would just keep paying for a storage unit of unknown items. There would never be a more perfect time. After the second visit, my mom didn't ask questions, and we didn't provide any extra information.

socks, mismatched Tupperware, eight boxes of mail, three boxes of shoes (some mismatched)

We developed a system, Angie and me. She sat outside in the early morning El Paso shade while I lifted and carried out dusty box after dusty box. Things quickly became clear. It was a repeat of cleaning out Ita's house. But instead of everything being wrapped in sadness, this time our emotions swung between awe at finding old family pictures, disgust at pulling out old aquarium rocks and pumps that hadn't been cleaned before they were stored, and laughter as we examined the '90s grunge clothing I'd left at home before moving.

clothes with tags still on them, a box of bath towels, two boxes of mismatched bedroom linens, a

In between trips we often yelled out, "Oh my god! Look!" or "Hey, do you want this?" On one of my back-and-forths, my sister called out to me—

box of random tools, a box of car and metal spare parts, a meat slicer, three plastic rolling bins

"Come here. Smell this."

In front of her sat a large moving box.

"Just smell it."

I bent over, half my body disappearing into the box, and breathed deeply.

"Mmmm . . . "

"What does it smell like?"

"Ita's bathroom."

"Avon's Skin So Soft!"

We laughed. The box was filled with my Ita's bathroom linens.

"What do we do with them?"

"Goodwill!"

"Yeah."

two ab machines, an electronic scooter, Home Interiors' décor still in the boxes, two boxes of

It took us three weeks of early-morning visits. We had to quit by early afternoon, or we'd be scorched by the sun and heat.

mystery novels, a box of stuffed animals, camping chairs, tent, and fishing poles, old lingerie

We'd leave, my car filled with things to sell on Craigslist and Angie's with stuff to donate to Goodwill. We threw dirty fish rocks, stiff throw rugs, and other things in the storage dumpster nearby. The manager at the storage place peeked out every time to remind us that the dumpster was for everyone who rented a unit. After a few trips home, Daniel asked if we were just moving the storage to our house. I'd spend the rest of the afternoon in the garage, snapping pics and posting ads to sell the workout equipment and random brass wall sconces as quickly as possible. I'd sneak the money into my mom's bank account after each sale. Mom didn't ask questions, and we didn't provide information.

work uniforms from when she worked on the bridge, twelve large black trash bags of miscellaneous

Mid-afternoon, we'd have breakfast at IHOP while most people were having lunch. We took turns going to the restaurant bathroom to wash our faces and arms. We left little brown trails of dirty water in the sink. At breakfast we were famished. I drank glass after glass of water.

"Man, how . . . does Mom have all these things?" I asked every time. Angie theorized, "She didn't like . . . she didn't want . . . she was afraid"—the list went on and on. Dealing with the things in the storage meant dealing with the things our mother avoided. Knowing that we would eventually take care of it was easier for her. The magnitude of all the things we found, donated, kept, sold, and threw away astounds me even today.

a box of various saints and a Buddha, award plaques from work, five stone

If Mom were to tell the story, it wouldn't be that bad. In her version of the story, she knew exactly what was in there, and we were just exaggerating. But she wasn't covered in dust, finding jars of rancid face creams we had to open to make sure she hadn't hidden jewelry in them or old stiff throw rugs filled with bug carcasses. To her, everything was fine. To her, not dealing with it made everything okay.

On our last trip to Goodwill, we filled the bed of my mom's gray 1992 Toyota pickup to the brim. The large oversized spare tire which was chained to the back stood precariously on the edge of the open bed.

"Will I make it?" Angie asked.

"Just go slow. I'll follow you. If it rolls out, it's chained. I'll honk. Let's just get this shit done, man," I said, wiping my forehead on the back of my forearm. I wore latex gloves to keep my hands clean and from touching unwanted things. They were caked with dust.

"Yeah. Yeah. We can do it." Angie hopped in the truck. We were off.

nesting coffee tables, four large blankets, two flat plastic storage bins filled with pajamas, a

We drove slowly down Montana. I turned on my hazards so people would go around. When we finally came to a stop, I held my breath as my sister pulled out. She turned onto George Dieter, another busy street.

The large tire rolled in, then out, right toward me.

It stayed in the truck though. We kept going. I kept my eyes on it and the mountain of things we'd arranged in the bed. The pile was so high, I couldn't see Angie. But I stayed close behind her. I cursed as we reached another light. *Come on!* She crept out into the intersection. In. Out.

The tire fell.

It dangled on the side of the truck and into the next lane. I honked, but Angie kept driving. I honked again. She drove. I reached for my phone and called.

"The tire fell!"

"What?"

"Yeah, I honked! It fell! It's hanging off the side of the truck!"

"I thought you honked telling me to go!"

"What? Why would I—pull over. I'll jump out and lift it in."

She pulled into the next turnoff. Cars zoomed by us. I put my car in park, jumped out, and ran toward the pick-up with the helpless tire hanging on its side. I squatted down, cradled the tire in my arms, thought *use your core*, and lifted. I got the tire about half-way up before I lost momentum. I dropped it and tried again. My tired body wasn't strong enough. My back already ached from loading and dumping boxes all day.

basketball, a yellow bicycle, an ammo box, two large speakers, a brown filing cabinet, three

"I *can't lift it! Angie!*" I yelled over the traffic. "*I can't lift it!*"

I couldn't see her, but somehow, she heard me or knew I was taking too long. She came around and stood on one side.

boxes of glasswear, one box of mismatched pans and lids, mismatched dumbbell weights

"Ready?" she asked.

THIRTY-SEVEN

I WENT TO my annual OBGYN exam. She gave me medical orders to get a mammogram. I was thirty-five years old. At the imaging office, as I filled out the paperwork, I got confused by the questions.

What was the first day of your last period?

When did your period stop?

I knew the answer to the first one. When the radiologist took me back, I had to ask her about the second one. She smiled at me and shook her head.

"That's for women who've gone through menopause," she said.

I felt my cheeks go warm. *Of course, it meant that.*

"You're pretty young to be getting a mammogram," she said.

I nodded and went into the story about my Ita. She nodded and listened as she placed my breasts between two hard clear plastic panes. Her brows creased when I shrieked from the pain of having my breast flattened into an unbreast-like shape.

"Shouldn't there be a better way to do this?" I asked,

cupping my breast once it was released from its flattened compressed position.

"Can you believe this is the same way they've been doing it since the '60s?" she asked, squishing my breast at a different angle.

"If men had to do this to their balls, they would have already come up with something different," I said through gritted teeth.

She laughed. When we were done, I joked about next time her buying me a drink at least. She made it as pleasant an experience as it could be.

Fast-forward two weeks. I received a phone call from the imaging office.

"Hi, Ms. Ramirez. This is Desert Imaging's office. We need to schedule an appointment to have some additional images done of your left breast. There isn't a reason for concern. Because you have dense breast tissue, we need to make sure we get a clearer image."

I got a call from my OBGYN's office saying the same thing. When I got home there was a letter telling me the same thing, only this time they said, "This is often not cancer."

This is often not cancer.

The only thing I saw was

Cancer

Cancer

Cancer

Cancer

I texted Angie, a nurse who would surely make me feel better, and asked if there was any reason to worry. Instead of reassuring me, she asked me a bunch of questions that only made me more nervous.

I had to wait a week before going in for a special appointment.

The warm radiologist who had squished me before was not there. In her place was a white woman who was all business and didn't laugh at my water-balloon jokes. This time the machine squeezed my left breast much harder than it had last time. With the second angle, tears sprung to my eyes, and I couldn't breathe from the pain. I thought of my Ita.

The third image was the worst, as the machine compacted not only my breast but my upper pectoral muscle. I thought of Ita's jagged scar.

But I still had one more stop. The doctor had requested a bilateral sonogram as well.

"Is dense breast tissue a bad thing?" I asked following her back to the waiting room.

"For someone your age, no. But it is for the images."

I nodded and sat back down in the waiting room. All the scars and faces of the women I had helped in my work flashed through my head. I thought of them going through this process. I thought of having to be naked in front of people and having their breasts machine-handled and contorted into shapes a breast should not be in. I thought of my Ita.

They called my name after twenty minutes. I went in and undressed once again. This time two women were in the room and, when I tried to make conversation, they gave yes or no answers. Compared to what I'd just endured, the sonogram was nothing.

"Why can't I just get a sonogram and not be pancaked?" I asked.

The woman prepping me for the procedure gave me an answer I didn't quite understand. She didn't smile at me once. Lying back with gel spread all over my breasts and an unsmiling woman pushing the sonogram scanner against me was better than the mammogram machine, but somehow it was a cold kind of intimacy.

When she was done, the other woman in the room walked out with the images in her hand. She left to show them to a faceless doctor I had never met. Is this how they tell women they have cancer?

I don't remember how many women I fit for bras. I don't know how many cancer survivors I helped. I remember only one who walked out without trying on anything.

"I can't do this," was all she said with hard eyes and a pinched face.

She was still mourning the loss of her breast and got angry at me. That was when I worked at the Hurst store. When she left, I picked up all the boxes and went to the backroom and cried for her loss and my Ita's.

I thought of this woman again. And I thought of the woman who had had a bilateral mastectomy who joked about running being so much easier. I thought of my Ita sitting in my same spot decades ago. I thought of the stories I heard of her mourning her breast. I thought of breasts and their purpose.

I thought and thought in what seemed to be the longest moment of holding my breath.

Then she came back in the room.

"The doctor said you're fine. You can go ahead and get cleaned up and dressed," she said with a smile.

It was the first smile. When the two women left the

room, I got up and reached for paper towels to rub the gel off my chest. I felt like I'd just had bad sex and was wiping away someone's sticky cum. I threw the paper towels in the garbage and got dressed. I put my sunglasses on even though I was still inside. As I walked out, no one said anything to me. I gave the women in the waiting room a fleeting glance as I exited the building.

The sun was bright, even with sunglasses. My steps quickened as I made way to my car. An older man nodded at me, but I passed him so quickly I didn't nod back. I hadn't parked far, but it felt like miles away. I fell into the driver's seat. A sob escaped my throat. The hot flash of tears ran down my cheeks, and I leaned over the steering wheel crying in the parking lot. I cried for the pain in my left breast that would still hurt five hours later. I cried for the women who sat in the waiting room, for the women at Nordstrom who allowed me to see their scarred naked bodies, for the woman who wrote me the thank-you card. But mostly, I cried for my Ita, who hadn't ever gotten over the loss of her breast. I cried for all the things these women went through, because today, I understood a little more.

I was lucky. I heard these words:

You're fine.

You're fine.

You're fine.

THIRTY-EIGHT

SOMETIME IN MAY 2015, Drew told me she was tired, and it was time for us to say goodbye. She was twenty.

Drew B saw so many things. Maybe more than she would have liked. As a kitten, I took her with me everywhere, in a backpack, until she threw up in a friend's car one day. She hated cars. Her first home was when we lived with Ita, then we moved back to the Eastside with Mom. She moved to Dallas with me and lived on the second floor of Angie's house, away from the dogs. We lived with a roommate after college, but that didn't last long. We quickly moved to our townhome, where we stayed until we moved back home to El Paso. We lived with Mom and Joe for a little while, then it was just us back at our Eastside home. We lived alone for a few years, but then Daniel moved in in 2013 and just like that, Drew had a dad.

She liked Daniel, and even though she was older and was starting to look a little grumpy, she liked that he sang to her, "Adventurous Drew! Adventurous Drew! Doesn't care about consequences!" Because she did get adventurous. Always an indoor cat, she escaped and went outside a few times and came back the next morning. One of those times, I found her waiting near my car after I'd searched the whole house and screamed her name up and down the block.

The night before she said goodbye, she followed me around the house. I tried to get her to eat, but she wouldn't. I even tried her favorite, French fries, but she just sniffed them and lay down in the middle of the kitchen. She never did that. She'd grown thin, and now, in retrospect, I think she'd let her new sister Sami, a rescue weenie dog, eat her special kidney food when I wasn't looking.

I slept in the living room with her that night. She couldn't jump down from the bed anymore, and I was afraid she'd have an accident, so we both slept on the floor in a makeshift bed of comforters. Drew was restless and paced before getting herself kind of comfortable. She didn't sleep much that night. Neither did I.

In the morning, Daniel and I took her to the vet. As we sat waiting, I talked to her a little. I told her how much I loved her, and that I was only doing this because she asked. Because she looked so unhappy now. Because she wouldn't eat. They knew her well there. She was one of their oldest cats. In human years, they estimated she was around 105.

After, we came home. Sami was waiting for us and sniffed for Drew. I cried so hard my head ached. Later that night, Daniel and I sat together in our bed.

"She is better now, you know?" he said again.

I nodded. My face was swollen from all the crying,

"Can I say something, and you won't think I'm crazy?"

He shook his head. "What?"

"I feel like Drew waited, you know? Until I was okay to," my voice cracked, "to leave."

Daniel hugged me. "Sure. She saw you had Sami—Sami and me. She could rest. She took care of you a long time."

THIRTY-NINE

1960s FLOOR MODEL RECORD PLAYER—$65 (EAST) Vintage 1960s floor model record player. Panels slide out and speakers light up with multicolored lights. Has been stored but is in working condition. OBO

Last week, I sold my grandma's tocadiscos. I posted an ad on Craigslist. The large wooden console sat in a storage unit and then the garage for years after we moved it out of her house.

It was dusty—tiny particles clung to the deeply carved details of the sliding doors as I snapped pictures of it with my cell phone. I remembered how it sat behind the front door with records and pictures and papers haphazardly stacked on top of it. I opened the sliding doors and pulled out the center holding the turntable, dials, and 8-track player. Dust also lined the ridges of the turntable. I snapped another picture and closed it back up. A few days later, I received a text from someone who wanted to buy it.

Julian, a teenager, showed up at my door with his uncle Hector. I was ready for them to take the record player, to help them load it in their truck, but Uncle Hector had questions for me.

"Does it work? Does it have tubes? Has it been in the family? When was the last time you used it?"

"Yes, it works. I don't know if it has tubes. It was my grandmother's. I'm not sure."

"Can we plug it in?"

I was still for a moment. I had never thought about having to plug it in. I thought surely they would just take the tocadiscos and leave.

As soon I plugged it in, I heard static through the speakers. Julian crouched in front of it and played with the dials, but nothing else came out.

"Here, let me try." I sat on the cool concrete floor of the garage.

I played with the dials, familiar yet unfamiliar because of all the years. When I flicked the switch to radio, a distant voice came on and the speakers lit up. Julian and his uncle began to talk about how they could fix it. Daniel stood with them, nodding. I glanced up and felt very small. I sat, legs crossed over each other, in front of my grandma's record player the same way I had when I was a child.

I turned back toward the dusty record player and suddenly I wasn't in my garage anymore. I was at home on California Street placing Javier Solís records with careful fingers on the round turntable. I stared at the speakers. They lit up green and red, and I remembered sitting for hours in front of them, watching as they changed to the sound of the songs.

Ita's house was never silent. Music was always at her

fingertips. She alternated between an old fuzzy radio that sat on her nightstand and the endless records she owned. She played records on one of the two large console record players in the house. My favorite had been this one because of the lights. I always sat and stared at the lights as she sang along and wondered why she wasn't on one of the records, making the lights dance.

While she cooked, she made up funny songs in Spanglish for me. I sat at the small round table in the brightly lit kitchen. She gave me small jobs like chopping onions, always warning me to be careful of my fingers. She sang "*En la calle de la araña . . .*" as she danced and hopped, her French twist coming loose while cooking our lunch of caldio. I laughed and begged her to stop.

Other times she'd put swing records on, and we'd sing and dance in the living room. We stepped and moved all around, slid across the wooden floor as the trumpets echoed, loud, in the house. We'd burst into laughter. My attempt to move as gracefully as she did was unsuccessful. I'd give up and just spin round and round, arms held out, my eyes entranced by the spinning dress around my knees while I made her laugh.

I thought about the tape I'd made of her singing at The Who's and the hum of the conversations that escalated with each sip of beer or cocktail. Ita's eyes were lit up from within as she sang. Each time, she gave away small pieces of herself that she never seemed to get back. That night, I managed to capture half a cassette of my grandma at her best. Her contagious laugh, her beautiful voice, and the memory of the look in her eyes as she sang, gazing at something I wanted so desperately to see.

"How much will you take for it?"

The uncle's voice broke into the memories that flooded back to me. I stared at the lights. They flickered the same way they had when I was little.

"How about fifty? Does that work?"

"Yes! We'll take it!" Julian broke through before his uncle could answer.

I turned back toward the dark wood of the tocadiscos and felt as if I were betraying her, selling her favorite record player for a measly fifty dollars, but then I saw Julian's face. His smile was so big. He could hardly stand still. He would love this record player, give it a future that I wouldn't have. It would play music again, the way my Ita would have wanted.

As I stood to get out of the way, I had to remind myself, *the tocadiscos is not my Ita.* I said it one more time as it was loaded in back of their minivan. I said it again as I took the fifty dollars from Uncle Hector, and I said it one last time as they drove away. Daniel pulled the garage door shut. Ah no . . . I felt the composure I'd been struggling to hold on to fade. The burn in my throat made its way into my nose. Daniel pulled me into his arms.

"I didn't think it would be so hard," I mumbled into his chest. "I know it's not my Ita, but . . ."

He nodded and pulled me close, letting me cry for something I'd lost years ago.

FORTY

I THINK THAT many writers and storytellers believe that the stories that don't want to be told—the ones that hurt down in the deep recesses of one's soul or bring a wave of embarrassment and regret—are the ones that need to be shared.

Part of me wants to yell out "*Why?!*"

Most of me does anyway, but then I realize that in this space I've created, I've shed light on many things about my grandma that she probably wouldn't have wanted shared. She can't do anything about it though. But the truth is, she does.

Months ago, I dreamt about her again. The dreams I have about her are fewer now than in the beginning, after her death, or even in the middle, when I lived in Dallas. I like to believe she thinks I need her less. I am happier now. I found a calling in the classroom and in front of a laptop doing this. Writing. Confessing. Storytelling. I have a husband my family firmly agrees she would have adored. I have furry pets that I'm crazy about. I am now a dog person. Can you believe it? Just ask my papito, Faustino, and chiquito, Doby. Two chihuahua rescues. Tino found us after being abandoned at a park a month after Drew left me. I think she told him he'd have a good home with us because he wouldn't leave after we shooed him. He just sat and stared.

But that night Ita came, and we were in church sitting in the front pews. It was a church I had never seen before. I was happy to see her. In my dream, I knew she'd been dead awhile now. We both knew. I don't remember what we said, but I know I told her I missed her. She seemed happy too. She was younger than in the last photos of her life. She was the Ita of my childhood. Spunky.

When we got up to leave, though, the dream took a dramatic shift. Instead of standing, she held her arm out to me. My Ita never had issues walking, but I shrugged and reached for her. That's when it happened. She was heavy. Deadweight. I placed her arms around my shoulders as if I were going to give her a piggyback ride, but I couldn't move. No matter how much I shifted or tugged, she remained a weight too heavy for me to carry. What did my Ita do?

She laughed.

I tried to grab hold of her. I pushed and pulled, but she was like a child, giggling.

"Ita, it's not funny," I said.

I repeated it over and over until I woke up. A nice visit from my Ita had taken a dark turn.

When I told my mom the dream the next day, she stayed quiet.

"What does it mean, Mom?" I asked.

The heaviness of it still hung around me. My Ita was there.

"Mija, I think it's time you finished her book. You keep waiting, writing more and stopping."

"What?"

"You started it because you felt guilty for not being there for her at the end, for not calling enough, for not seeing her before . . . she died. She knew, she understood. You had to live your life. You can't carry her forever."

The last part echoed for days.

You can't carry her forever.

But if I finish, have I completed my penance? If I finish, will I lose her again?

My great friend and unofficial editor gave me *The Art of Memoir* by Mary Karr a couple months ago. In reading it, I found a quote I immediately liked and felt as if she were speaking directly to me. "No matter how self-aware you are, memoir wrenches at your insides precisely because it makes you battle with your very self—your neat analyses and tidy excuses." No truer words have ever been spoken.

It's been several years since I really began to focus on this story of my Ita. Each time I think I'm done, there are more questions than answers. I think a part of me wants to be done because I'm tired of having my insides wrenched. Or, to be honest, maybe there are aspects that haven't been wrenched enough.

In this memoir, where I want to focus on my Ita, there is a light that inevitably wants to shine on me because I am as much a character as she is. I am just as important even though I want to stay backstage and let her bask in the limelight. I must learn to be in the light and also be the stagehand pulling the levers and changing the lighting. I have to be both. I have to get comfortable showing just as much of myself as I've shown of her.

She is beckoning me onstage. "Ándale, Prieta," she says. But suddenly I am seven years old again, and I want to hide behind the word-filled pages of her life as easily as I hid behind her legs as a child. But I've had to edit, revise, and write myself next to her in that limelight. In this space, we can still be together.

AFTERWORD

MY GREAT-GREAT-GRANDFATHER FRANCISCO Acosta was born in Saucillo, Chihuahua, Mexico in 1882. In 1888, he emigrated with his family to El Paso, Texas. He was still a child and they were searching for opportunity on the other side. He grew up in what was a small dusty town of around 10,000 people at the time. It was here he met Maria Sosa. She was from Juárez, México just across the Rio Grande River. At that time, there were no walls. The first bridge had just been built a few years before. A simple flatboat ferry could be taken from one side of the river to the other.

El Paso's landscape changed with the arrival of the railroad, and Francisco, a laborer, took advantage of the boom. At that time, Asarco Railroad and Mining was one of the first transnational corporations. Its success depended on the relations between the sister cities. This drew people looking for work. Between 1890 and 1910, the city's population more than tripled from 10,000 to almost 40,000 people. The desert town started to see more movement and travelers. This bustle somehow brought Francisco and

Maria together, and in 1904, they welcomed the first of six children, my great-grandfather Alfredo Acosta.

My great-grandfather Alfredo owned a filling station on Piedras and what would later become Grant Avenue. We don't know what happened to the filling station because, after a while, he worked as a taxi driver. I only met him once, near the time of his death. I was three years old, but his thick silver hair and light, almost yellowish-brown eyes are burned in my memory. Ita sat next to his bed in a small room of the home he made with his second wife. I hovered in the doorway, watching how his face lit up when he saw her. Ita glowed even though she knew the end was coming. She was always his favorite. His *manocucha*—a term of endearment he came up with because she was a lefty.

My great-great-grandmother Manuela was born in Texas. At a very young age, she married Pedro Davila and gave birth to my great-grandmother Guadalupe Davila in 1908. I don't know anything about Pedro Davila. What I do know is Manuela left Guadalupe with her parents when Guadalupe was a child. They lived somewhere in Mexico. She remarried a man named Pascual Ortiz and always seemed to be on the move. Guadalupe had a quiet, solitary childhood with her grandparents. Manuela sent dolls as gifts for her daughter from her travels with Pascual, but instead of being able to play with them, they were hung on her bedroom wall. Dolls were to be admired, not played with. Guadalupe was a child in an adult's world, and Manuela was having too much fun to stop and be the mother she needed.

On January 31, 1928, Guadalupe married Alfredo Acosta. She was nineteen years old. They had four children of their own. Alicia Acosta, my Ita, was the second youngest. Guadalupe was a homemaker and loved all her children, but there must have been flashes of her own mother, Manuela, in Ita, because as a child she was sent away to live with her madrina, her godmother, in California.

Ita became the lone girl in a family of four boys, so she adapted. She borrowed a pair of pants, when girls only wore dresses, looped a rope through the belt loops and learned to box, play marbles, and overall roughhouse. She became one of the boys and stayed with her madrina several years. When she finally came back to El Paso, to Segundo Barrio, she felt out of place. She spoke more English now, while everyone spoke Spanish. Her two older sisters were strangers. She was put back in dresses. One of her comforts was her younger brother since they could play together. Her father seemed to be the only one with a face full of smiles for her. When he wasn't working, he played guitar while she sang. Still, Ita didn't fit, and no matter what she did, her mother's face remained unsmiling.

Ita worked as an elevator operator at the once beautiful downtown Caples Building. She met a man named Manuel Lopez there.

As she pushed buttons for people, he smiled and said, "You're going to be my wife."

Ita scoffed, "I don't even know you."

Ita married him when she was twenty. They moved to Los Angeles. Ita was tired of unsmiling faces. Mamá Lupe didn't approve of Manuel or of the marriage and called Ita a whore when she became pregnant with Leticia, my mom. Even in another state, Ita couldn't shake Mamá Lupe's disapproval. Ita did the best she could when she discovered Manuel was not her knight in shining armor. Knights don't beat women. She did her best for most of her life, even when it wasn't always the best.

Leticia, my mom, worked as a mechanic at Southwestern Bell and had a nine-year-old daughter, Angie, when she met my dad, Jesús. She was twenty-six. They met at a bar, the Hideaway, where Ita worked at the time. He made a living as a carpenter, making countertops and cabinets with his brother. He was divorced and had three children of his own, a girl around Angie's age and two boys. So Angie didn't scare him away. Ita glared at him, a stout barrel of a man with an arched brow and thin lips. Mom married him September 1979. By 1981, they were separated. Mom said they got along fine as long as they didn't live together, so that's just what they did. On weekends, we were a family. But when Mom got laid off from the phone company and left for Customs training in Georgia, she left us with Ita, not my dad. In 1989, Mom made it official and filed for divorce from a marriage that hadn't really been a marriage.

So where am I from?

I come from Francisco and Maria, Manuela and Pedro, Guadalupe and Alfredo, Alicia and Manuel, Leticia and Jesús: a long line of people who also pursued a better life. And I live in the largest and oldest border town in the United States, El Paso. El Chuco to locals. Its land once belonged to Mexico, but even when it changed owners, its roots, las raíces, remained Mexican. My skin is still brown because the land is still brown, and even the gringo transplants who move here—professors at UTEP, Fort Bliss military, or customs agents—start to turn a little brown too. La cultura is a marriage of those two things. Mexican and American, Spanish and English, tacos al pastor and Texas-sized steaks.

My family is all these things, and this is *our* story.

MY ITA'S RECIPES

EL CALDIO

"When you miss Ita, make this caldio she made you as a child."

Prep Time: 15 minutes
Cook Time: 30 minutes
Servings: 5

Ingredients:

1 tablespoon vegetable oil
1 onion, chopped
2 garlic cloves, minced
1 pound beef stew meat
1 can mixed vegetables
1 can tomato sauce
3 cups water
Salt and pepper to taste

Directions:

1. Heat oil in a large cast iron skillet over medium-

high heat. Add onions and garlic. Stir occasionally until onions are soft. Try not to cry with the scent of garlic and onion sizzling, reminding you of your childhood spent in a cramped yellow kitchen chopping onions before they went in the pan.

2. Add in stew meat and continue cooking until it is browned. Stir it by flicking your wrist clockwise or else it will stick, and you'll have big clumps of beef, onion, and garlic, like the ones stuck in your throat the day you vomited cleaning out Ita's house.

3. Put the meat mixture into a soup pot. Be careful not to burn yourself. You're not sure what to put on burns since you found out butter smeared on the wound, like your grandma used to do, isn't really the right remedy.

4. Add in a can of mixed vegetables and a can of tomato sauce. Be sure to rinse the leftover tomato sauce from the can before you throw it away—it's wasteful to leave any sauce in the can—and pour in about 3 cups of water, more or less, depending on if you want it more caldoso, soupy, or mas espeso, thicker, like a stew—and bring to a boil. Salt and pepper to taste, but remember too much salt isn't good for you.

Cook's Notes:

The caldio is easy to make and will last for days.

You can also add chile for flavor. When you eat this, you'll be able to taste the yellow kitchen and feel the warmth of your grandma's hands as she helped you scoop the onions into the black cast-iron pan.

LOS TACOS DE ITA

"When you want to share a bit of home, and your childhood, make these for guests. They will taste like Ita's love."

Prep Time: 30 minutes
Cook Time: 45 minutes
Servings: 4-5
Serving size: 3 tacos

Ingredients:

Tacos
1 large or 2 medium russet potatoes
½ small white onion, chopped finely
2 dientes de ajo, garlic teeth, minced
1 pound lean carne molida, ground beef
1 teaspoon of cumin
Salt and pepper to taste
1 package corn tortillas from your favorite tortilleria
Oil for frying

Toppings
2 vine-ripe tomates, cut into small wedges
½ onion, sliced
2 cups muenster cheese, grated
½ head iceberg lechuga, chopped
Chile de árbol

Directions:

1. Slice the papas into chunks and put to boil until

falling-apart tender. The first time you made these, you didn't do that, and they didn't mash easily into the ground beef. Instead of blending, the tacos were lumpy.

2. Put the chopped onions and garlic to cook in a smidge of oil. This is your childhood smell. Anything that was ever delicious started with this scent. When you make these for people, you can tell who grew up in a household that loved to cook because they gravitate to the kitchen to "talk" but really, they are just there to breathe in the scent of an onion-and-garlic home.

3. Add ground beef and season with salt, pepper, and cumin. Don't put in too much cumin or your axilas, armpits, will smell the next day.

4. Drain the water from the potatoes and add them to the ground beef. Mix it all well until the meat and papas are a kind of soft mush. Remove from heat. You will remember hovering in the kitchen when Ita made these because they were your favorite. She would shoo you away from the edge of the stove so she could cook in peace.

5. In a kitchen towel, warm 5-8 tortillas in the microwave for about 45 seconds. This will keep the tortillas from cracking when you put them in the oil. Warm a batch at a time, so they don't cool while the tacos crisp in the oil. Ita used to heat them on the gas stove, her fingertips impermeable to the blue flames. Even though you cook often, your fingertips are not impermeable. You cheat.

6. Once warm, use a tablespoon to scoop the papa carne mixture into the tortilla and place into a pan with heated oil. Use a cast-iron pan. They taste better. When you made

them in Miami for your in-laws, they didn't have a cast-iron. You could taste the difference, but they are Colombian. They don't know. They ate taco after taco. When a tía put ketchup on Ita's tacos, you wanted to slap it out of her hand. Instead, you frowned and ran inside from the patio. They noticed.

7. Brown each side to your liking. Repeat for the rest of the papa carne mixture. Place cooked tacos on a cooking sheet lined with napkins to absorb excess oil.

8. Others following this recipe must find a red salsa at their local tienda because you are forbidden from sharing the recipe for Ita's chile de árbol. It is famous. A friend begs for the recipe. Even though you've known each other since high school, you refuse. The chile needs to be red and spicy though. Eso le da el sabor. The flavor.

9. Place cooked tacos, toppings, and salsa on the table. Each person can make their tacos, al gusto, as they please. Each time you make these tacos, watch people's faces. You will remember Ita telling you the recipe over the phone when you moved to Dallas. You will be grateful for this memory.

Cook's Notes:

People will eat more than usual. You've never seen someone just eat three.

Ita never got to travel much. Now, she's gone many places through her tacos. You've taken her to Dallas, Texas; Miami, Florida; and Medellín, Colombia. Twice you've made the tacos in Medellín. You traveled with a bag of chile de arbol from Texas because Colombians aren't spicy people. No les gustan picante. But the tacos aren't Ita's if they don't have even a little spice.

When you make these, you will be able to share stories of your childhood with Ita. Instead of crying, you laugh and smile now because you will be able to share a bit of her, and she will be remembered. Just the way she always hoped.

ACKNOWLEDGMENTS

THIS BOOK—MY FIRST—BEGAN as way to grieve, but it also led me down a path to people who helped and guided me to where it is today.

I am grateful to Lee Byrd and la familia Byrd for believing in me and my story. They invited me into their Cinco Puntos Press home. I'm honored to have their faith in my work, and to be in the company of the many other prestigious authors they've published. Becky Powers showed me the way when I was lost in the story, and Jessica Powers helped me sharpen and refine its lens. Thank you to Anne Giangiulio, who designed the cover. I'm still speechless at how fate connected us. The women we lost brought us together for a reason. I'm grateful to Stephanie Frescas Macías for all her promotion ideas to help shine a light on the book, and for answering all my newbie questions about the publishing process.

I am thankful to Lex Williford for helping to nurture the book when it was still a thesis called "Por Un Amor." To Dr. Meredith Abarca for reminding me about my love for food and of cooking with Ita. Many, many thanks to the Creative Writing Faculty at the University of Texas of El Paso and graduate cohort for helping a shy writer come out of her shell.

I couldn't have kept chugging along in this process if it wasn't for writers and dear friends Sylvia Aguilar, Minerva Laveaga, and Richard Yañez, each ever patient but always nudging. I can't forget

Sarah Stayton and Ignacio Troncoso, my forever besties and blurb readers, who let me send slices and paragraphs via Messenger to ask, "Does this make sense?"

There will never be a big enough thank-you for my family. They have answered all my questions. Even though they heard bits and pieces about what I was doing, they never asked me to stop. Mom, Angie, Tío, and Gabe, thank you for supporting me in sharing our stories with strangers. I'm forever grateful for your unwavering support.

Finally, to my photographer, webmaster, champion, sous chef, best friend, and partner Daniel. Each time I hit a bump, you let me cry, mourn, but you never let me stop. You are my favorite person and salsero.

Ita would have loved you.

Photo by Daniel Ríos Lopera

YASMÍN RAMÍREZ IS the 2020 recipient of the Woody and Gayle Hunt-Aspen Institute Fellowship Award as well as a 2018 Dickinson House Fellow. Her fiction and creative nonfiction works have appeared in *Cream City Review* and *Huizache,* among others. She is an Assistant Professor at El Paso Community College, where she teaches English, Creative Writing, and Chicanx Literature. She stays active in the El Paso literary community and serves on the board of BorderSenses, a literary non-profit. *¡Ándale, Prieta!* is her first book. Please visit her website at yasminramirez.com.